The Agricultural Link: How Environmental Deterioration Could Disrupt Economic Progress

LESTER R. BROWN

Jennifer D. Mitchell, *Staff Researcher*

WORLDWATCH PAPER 136
August 1997

FINANCIAL SUPPORT for the Institute is provided by the Nathan Cummings Foundation, the Geraldine R. Dodge Foundation, The Ford Foundation, the Foundation for Ecology and Development, The William and Flora Hewlett Foundation, W. Alton Jones Foundation, John D. and Catherine T. MacArthur Foundation, Charles Stewart Mott Foundation, The Curtis and Edith Munson Foundation, The Pew Charitable Trusts, Rockefeller Brothers Fund, Rockefeller Financial Services, Summit Foundation, Turner Foundation, U.N. Population Fund, Wallace Genetic Foundation, Wallace Global Fund, and the Weeden Foundation.

THE WORLDWATCH PAPERS provide in-depth, quantitative and qualitative analysis of the major issues affecting prospects for a sustainable society. The Papers are written by members of the Worldwatch Institute research staff and reviewed by experts in the field. Published in five languages, they have been used as concise and authoritative references by governments, nongovernmental organizations, and educational institutions worldwide. For a partial list of available Papers, see back pages.

Printed on 100-percent non-chlorine bleached, partially recycled paper.

Table of Contents

Agriculture: The Missing Link 5

Demand Outrunning Supply 9

Land and Water Scarcity 19

A Century of Yield Takeoffs 32

Raising Grain Yields 38

Facing Biological Reality 46

The Emerging Politics of Scarcity 51

An Unprecedented Challenge 59

Notes 65

Tables and Figures

Table 1: *Wheat Yield Per Hectare in Key Producing*
　　　Countries, 1995 41

Table 2: *Rice Yield Per Hectare in Key Producing Countries, 1995* 42

Table 3: *Corn Yield Per Hectare in Key Producing Countries, 1995* ... 45

Table 4: *Annual Change in World Grain Yields by Decade, 1950–95* . 47

Figure 1: *World Production of Animal Protein by Source, 1950–96* .. 11

Figure 2: *China: Grain Used for Feed, 1950–97* 13

Figure 3: *World Grain Production Per Person, 1950–96* 15

Figure 4: *World Grain Carryover Stocks, as Days of Consumption,*
　　　1961–97 17

Figure 5: *World Wheat Price, 1950–96* 18

Figure 6: *World Soybean Area, 1950–96* 23

Figure 7: *Grain Area Per Person, 1950–96, With Projections*
　　　to 2030 25

Figure 8: *Saudi Arabia Grain Production, 1960–96* 29

Figure 9: *World Irrigated Area Per Person, 1950–95, With Projections to 2030* 31

Figure 10: *World Grain Yield Per Hectare, 1950–96* 32

Figure 11: *Rice Yield for Japan (1878–1996) and Wheat Yield for United States (1866–1996)* 33

Figure 12: *World Fertilizer Use, 1950–96* 37

Figure 13: *Wheat Yields in France, China, and the United States, 1950–96* 39

Figure 14: *Rice Yields in Japan, China, and India, 1950–96* 43

Figure 15: *Corn Yields in the United States, China, and Brazil, 1950–96* 46

Figure 16: *U.S. Grain Yield Per Hectare, 1950–96* 53

The views expressed are those of the author and do not necessarily represent those of the Worldwatch Institute; of its directors, officers, or staff; or of its funding organizations.

ACKNOWLEDGMENTS: Reah Janise Kauffman helped me with the paper through several drafts, providing useful commentary and feedback along the way. Jennifer Mitchell provided strong research support, making the production of the paper much easier than it otherwise would have been. Among those who gave generously of their time to review all or parts of the paper are Dana Dalrymple, Donald Duvick, Gary Gardner, William H. Mansfield III, Jim Perry, Sandra Postel, and Vernon Ruttan. Liz Doherty, our in-house designer, who readied it for the printer, was a delight to work with.

We are indebted to the Rasmussen Foundation and the Winslow Foundation for their financial support of our work on food security.

LESTER R. BROWN is founder, president, and a senior researcher at the Worldwatch Institute. The senior author of the Institute's two annuals, *State of the World* and *Vital Signs*, he is perhaps best known for his pioneering work on the concept of environmentally sustainable development.

Agriculture: The Missing Link

The trends of environmental deterioration of the last few decades cannot continue indefinitely without eventually affecting the world economy. Until now, most of the economic effects of environmental damage have been local: the collapse of a fishery here or there from overfishing, the loss of timber exports by a tropical country because of deforestation, or the abandonment of cropland because of soil erosion. But as the scale of environmental damage expands, it threatens to affect the global economy as well.

The consequences of environmental degradation are becoming more clear. We cannot continue to deforest the earth without experiencing more rainfall runoff, accelerated soil erosion, and more destructive flooding. If we continue to discharge excessive amounts of carbon into the atmosphere, we will eventually face economically disruptive climate change. If we continue to overpump the earth's aquifers, we will one day face acute water scarcity.

If we continue to overfish, still more fisheries will collapse. If overgrazing continues, so, too, will the conversion of rangeland into desert. Continuing soil erosion at the current rate will slowly drain the earth of its productivity. If the loss of plant and animal species continues at the rate of recent decades, we will one day face ecosystem collapse.

Everyone agrees that these trends can not continue indefinitely. But why not? Will they stop because we get our act together and do what we know we should do, but that politically we have so far not been able to do? Or will they not continue because they begin to disrupt the economic expansion that is causing their decline?

If these trends disrupt economic growth, how will they do it? What will the mechanism be? The thesis of this paper is that the food system is likely to be the sector through which environmental deterioration eventually translates into economic decline. This should not come as a surprise. Archeological evidence indicates that agriculture has often been the link between environmental deterioration and economic decline. The decline of the early Mesopotamian civilization was tied to the waterlogging and salting of its irrigated land. Soil erosion converted into desert the fertile wheatlands of North Africa that once supplied the Roman empire with grain. The Mayan civilization that flourished from 600 B.C. to 900 A.D. in the lowlands of Guatemala eventually declined, apparently because deforestation and soil erosion reduced the food supply, creating unmanageable food scarcity and political conflict.

According to the scenario outlined here, rising grain prices are likely to be the first global economic indicator to tell us that we are on an economic and demographic path that is environmentally unsustainable. If the trends of environmental damage just described continue unimpeded, they will seriously impair the capacity of fishers and farmers to keep up with the growth in demand, leading to rising food prices. As the social consequences of rising grain prices become unacceptable to more and more people, they are likely to lead to political instability. What begins as environmental degradation eventually translates into political instability.

A doubling of grain prices, such as occurred briefly for wheat and corn in early 1996, would not have a major immediate effect on the world's affluent, both because they spend only a small share of their income for food and because their food expenditures are dominated more by processing costs than by commodity prices. But for the 1.3 billion in the world who live on a dollar a day or less, a prolonged period of higher grain prices would quickly become life-threatening. Heads of households unable to buy enough food to keep their families alive would hold their governments responsible, and would likely take to the streets. The resulting bread or rice riots could disrupt economic activity in many countries. If the world could not get inflated food prices back down to traditional levels, this could negatively affect the earnings of multinational corporations, the performance of stock markets, and the stability of the international monetary system. In a world economy more integrated than ever before, the problems of the poor would then become the problems of the rich.[1]

The consequences of environmental abuse that scientists have warned about can be seen on every hand. The members of the European Union (EU) agreed in April 1997 to reduce the fish catch in many of the region's fisheries by 20 percent or more in an effort to avert their collapse. In Saudi Arabia, overreliance on a fossil aquifer to expand grain production contributed to an abrubt 62-percent drop in the grain harvest between 1994 and 1996. In the United States, record temperatures and crop-withering heat waves,

What begins as environmental degradation eventually translates into political instability.

which are likely the result of the buildup in greenhouse gases, reduced the grain harvest in three of the last nine years.[2]

In Kazakstan, the largest grain producer in central Asia, the Institute of Soil Management projects a loss of 30 percent of the country's grainland because of severe soil erosion. In China, where acute water scarcity now drains the Huang He (Yellow River) dry before it reaches the sea for part of every year, farmers face heavy cutbacks in irrigation. The soil degradation and resulting cropland abandonment that invariably follows the burning off of the Amazon rainforest for agriculture has helped make Brazil the largest grain importer in the western hemisphere.[3]

No one of these developments alone threatens world food security, but as the number of such situations multiplies, it becomes more and more difficult to feed a world population that is expanding by 80 million people per year. Even without further environmental degradation, we approach the new millennium with 800 million hungry and malnourished people.[4]

These 800 million are hungry because they are too poor to buy enough food to satisfy their basic nutritional needs, but if the price of grain were to double, as it already has for some types of seafood, it could impoverish hundreds of millions more almost overnight. In short, a steep rise in grain prices could impoverish more people than any event in history, including the ill-fated Great Leap Forward in China that led to the death by starvation of 30 million people between 1959 and 1961.[5]

The handful of examples just cited of how the degradation of the earth is beginning to threaten food security are but a few instances among thousands. Evidence that this could lead to food scarcity has been accumulating for many years. The oceanic fish catch, for example, plagued by overfishing and pollution, has grown little after increasing from 19 million tons in 1950 to 89 million tons in 1989. Grainland productivity increased by more than 2 percent a year from 1950 to 1990, but dropped to scarcely 1 percent a year from 1990 to 1995—well below the growth in demand.[6]

All the key food security indicators signal a shift from surplus to scarcity. During the mid-1990s the United States returned to use all the cropland that had been idled under commodity programs in an effort to offset the slower rise in land productivity. Even so, in 1996 world carryover stocks of grain, perhaps the most sensitive indicator of food security, dropped to the lowest level on record—a mere 52 days of consumption. Even with the exceptional harvest of 1996, stocks were rebuilt to only 57 days of consumption, far below the 70 days needed to provide a minimal buffer against a poor harvest. If grain stocks cannot be rebuilt with an outstanding harvest, when can they be?[7]

Food scarcity may provide the environmental wakeup call the world has long needed. Rising food prices may indicate the urgency of reversing the trends of environmental degradation before resulting political instability reaches the point where economic progress is no longer possible.

During the late spring and early summer of 1996, world wheat and corn prices set record highs under pressure from a 1995 harvest reduced by heat waves in the U.S. Corn Belt and China's emergence as the world's second largest grain importer. Wheat traded at over $7 a bushel, more than double the price in early 1995. In mid-July, corn traded at an all-time high of $5.54 a bushel, also double the level of a year earlier.[8]

In the summer of 1996, the government of Jordan, suffering from higher prices for imported wheat and a growing fiscal deficit, was forced to eliminate the bread subsidy. The resulting bread riots lasted several days and threatened to bring down the government.[9]

When scarcity raised grain prices by some 60 percent in China in 1994, Beijing responded to potential unrest, such as that which followed food price rises in 1989 and contributed to the Tiananmen Square demonstrations, by importing record amounts of grain, including wheat, rice, and corn. With a long national history of rising food prices translating into peasant unrest and revolt, an alarmed government moved quickly, becoming almost overnight the world's second largest grain importer.[10]

Several trends are converging to raise prices. With all oceanic fisheries being fished at or beyond capacity, farmers can no longer count on the world's fishing fleets to help them expand the food supply. With little new cropland to bring under the plow, future food security depends on raising land productivity. This in turn is complicated by the spreading scarcity of fresh water.

Demand Outrunning Supply

All the basic indicators of food security—grain production per person, seafood catch per person, carryover stocks of grain, cropland set aside, seafood and grain prices—signal a tightening situation during the 1990s. The growth in food production is slowing while the growth in demand, driven by population growth and rising affluence, continues to be strong.

Although global population growth has slowed somewhat during the 1990s, dropping to 1.4 percent in 1996, the world is continuing to add 80 million people a year because the population base is expanding. Providing for population growth alone now requires an expansion in the world grain harvest of 26 million tons a year.[11]

In recent years, incomes have risen far more rapidly in developing countries than in industrial ones, largely because growth is slowing in the latter as these nations approach industrial maturity. Meanwhile, economies in the developing world are growing rapidly, led by the extraordinarily rapid income growth in Asia, where more than half the world lives. Among low-income people, much of the growth in income goes to diversify diets. Rich people consume roughly four times as much grain as poor people do. In a country like India, only some 200 kilograms of grain are available per person, so nearly all of them must be consumed directly just to satisfy basic caloric needs. The average American, in contrast, uses roughly 800 kilograms of grain a year, most of them consumed indirectly in the form of beef, pork, poultry, eggs, milk, cheese, yogurt, and ice cream.[12]

The growing protein intensity of world diets is driving the demand for grain up at a rapid rate. A kilogram of beef added in the feedlot requires roughly 7 kilograms of grain; a kilogram of pork needs 4 kilograms; a kilogram of eggs, roughly 3 kilograms; a kilogram of poultry, just over 2 kilograms; and a kilogram of fish produced in a pond, just under 2 kilograms.[13]

The strong human appetite for animal protein is evident in the trends in Figure 1. Supplies of two of the leading sources of animal protein in the human diet, seafood and beef, essentially depend on natural systems. The seafood catch increased from 19 million tons at mid-century to 89 million tons in 1989, but has shown little growth since then, fluctuating around 90 million tons during the 1990s. A simi-

FIGURE 1

World Production of Animal Protein by Source, 1950–96

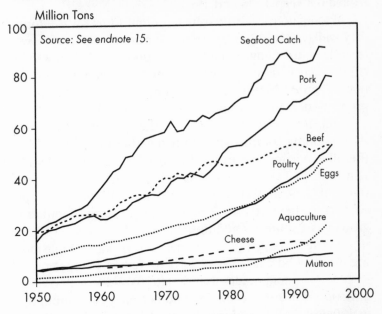

Million Tons

Source: See endnote 15.

lar picture emerges with beef: after increasing 2.5-fold from 1950 until 1990, production has increased little. With growth in the supplies of these two traditionally important sources of animal protein slowing down, the world is turning to other sources—pork, poultry, eggs, and farmed fish. The rapid growth in world pork production since the late 1970s is largely the result of the rise in affluence in China, where pork consumption per person has eclipsed that in the United States.[14]

Both poultry and egg consumption have also risen rapidly over the last two decades, partly because chickens are among the most efficient animals in converting grain into protein. Indeed, poultry production overtook beef in 1996 for the first time in history. Egg production has risen rapidly over the last decade, largely because eggs are not as dependent on refrigeration as meat and milk are. Thus in developing countries, where incomes are starting to rise but where refrigeration is not yet widespread, eggs have become a favorite source of animal protein. The other fast-growing source of animal protein is aquaculture, where production tripled between 1985 and 1995.[15]

Production levels of animal protein in its diverse forms vary widely. World production of beef from 1990 to 1996 was essentially unchanged. Pork production, led by growth in China, increased by 15 percent during this period. Meanwhile, poultry production jumped by some 32 percent. And egg production, climbing almost as fast, rose by 25 percent.[16]

All these trends are driven by the rapid rise in incomes in developing countries mentioned earlier. Gains in Asia, in the oil-exporting countries of North Africa and the Middle East, and in Latin America have been particularly impressive. But those in Asia have been the strongest of all. In some countries there, rising affluence is rivaling population growth as a source of additional demand for grain.

There is no historical precedent for so many people moving up the food chain so fast. When Western Europe entered its period of rapid modernization after World War II, creating a modern consumer economy and boosting consumption of grainfed livestock products, it had 280 million people. The United States, which was developing a grain-based livestock and poultry economy at the same time, had 160 million people. Today, Asia—from Pakistan east through Japan—has 3.1 billion people, more than half the world total. Excluding Japan, the economy of this region grew by some 8 percent a year from 1991 to 1996, much faster than the growth achieved earlier by either Western Europe or North America.[17]

Economic growth in Asia is led by China, where per capita income climbed by nearly four fifths between 1990 and 1996. Much of this additional income is translating into demand for more livestock products. During this time China's grain consumption increased by some 40 million tons, with more than 30 million tons of this growth consumed as feed. Between 1978, when economic reforms were adopted in China, and 1997, the grain used to feed livestock, poultry, and fish increased from less than 20 million tons to more than 100 million. (See Figure 2.)[18]

FIGURE 2

China: Grain Used for Feed, 1950–97

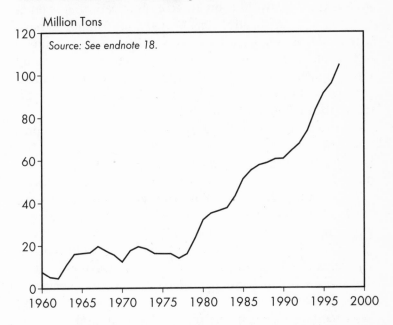

Million Tons

Source: See endnote 18.

China is not alone in moving up the food chain. In India, where the economy has expanded 6 percent a year during the mid-1990s, the broiler industry is growing by 15 percent annually. Egg consumption is rising at 3 percent a year. Milk consumption is also rising. The broiler industry in Indonesia, a country of 200 million people, is doubling every five years. Feedgrain use is climbing in almost every country in Asia—China, India, Indonesia, Malaysia, Pakistan, the Philippines, South Korea, Thailand, and Viet Nam.[19]

In addition, many countries are now importing beef, pork, and poultry directly. Japan imports close to two thirds of the beef it consumes. Beef imports into the Philippines and Indonesia are rising steadily. And China and Japan are two of the world's three leading poultry importers, along with Russia.[20]

Combined with population growth, this record rise in affluence for such a huge segment of humanity helps explain both why world grain surpluses are being replaced by scarcity and why future rises in grain prices could make it clear that the world is on an economic path that is environmentally unsustainable. Asia's grain imports have increased from some 6 million tons in 1950 to more than 90 million tons in 1995. Some Asian countries, including Japan, South Korea, and Taiwan, now import more than 70 percent of the grain they consume. Asia is becoming industrially strong, but agriculturally vulnerable.[21]

At the same time, the growing appetite for marine protein is outrunning the capacity of the oceans to satisfy it. From 1950 to 1989, when the oceanic fish catch was increasing 4.6-fold, the catch per person climbed from just under 8 kilograms to 17 kilograms. With the catch leveling off since 1989, the catch per person has started to decline, falling some 9 percent since then as population has continued to grow.[22]

The period from 1950 to 1989 witnessed both remarkable advances in technology and an impressive growth in the investment in fishing trawlers and factory processing ships, which enabled the exploitation of fisheries in the most remote corners of the planet. At 89 million tons, the oceanic catch of fish exceeded the combined production of beef and mutton on the world's rangelands. Seafood became an important source of animal protein, particularly for people living in island countries and in continental countries with long coastlines—augmenting diets otherwise dominated by starchy staples such as rice, corn, wheat, cassava, and other tropical root crops.[23]

From 1950 until roughly 1990, the additional fish catch of nearly 2 million tons a year helped satisfy the growing demand for animal protein. Now, however, relying on fish farming or broiler production to satisfy the continuing growth in the demand for animal protein that was once met by the oceans will require roughly 4 million additional tons of grain per year, putting even more pressure on the earth's land and water resources.[24]

While growth in the harvest from the oceans has come to a near standstill during the 1990s, that in the harvest from the land has continued, but at a much slower rate than during the preceding decades. From 1950 to 1990, the world grain harvest increased from 631 million tons to 1.78 billion tons, nearly tripling. This was a remarkable period in history, one in which rapidly growing demand stimulated production increases as farmers drew on a huge backlog of technology developed during the preceding century.[25]

Since 1990, however, the growth in the grain harvest has slowed dramatically. After expanding at close to 3 percent a year from 1950 to 1990, the harvest increased only 1 percent annually between 1990 and 1996. Signs of slower growth were already evident in the late 1980s as the growth in grain production fell below that of population, dropping the harvest per person from the all-time high of 342 kilograms in 1984 to 335 kilograms in 1990, a fall of 2 percent. By 1996, the harvest per person had fallen to 321 kilograms, declining an additional 4 percent. (See Figure 3.)[26]

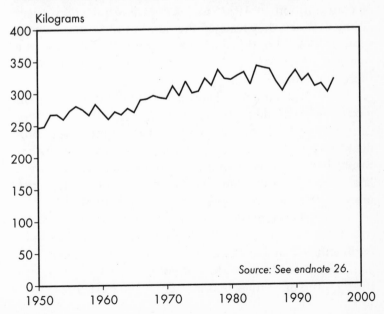

FIGURE 3

World Grain Production Per Person, 1950–96

Source: See endnote 26.

With this loss of momentum in the growth in the world grain harvest, it comes as no surprise that world grain stocks during the 1990s have dropped to their lowest level ever. The bumper harvests of the mid-1980s boosted carryover stocks for 1987 to more than 100 days of consumption. But since then they have dropped below 60 days of consumption. (See Figure 4.)[27]

In response to the tightening grain situation, the United States dismantled the commodity programs designed to support prices by holding land out of production; in 1996, farmers planted the land that had been set aside. Yet even with this additional land and with unusually favorable weather worldwide, there was little rebuilding of stocks from the 1996 harvest.[28]

Stocks that will provide at least 70 days of world consumption are needed for even a minimal level of food security. Without this, even one poor harvest can lead to sharp rises in grain prices. Whenever stocks fall below 60 days' worth, prices become highly volatile. With the margin of security so thin, grain prices fluctuate with each weather report. When carryover stocks of grain dropped to 56 days of consumption in 1973, for example, world grain prices doubled. When they reached the new low of 52 days of consumption in 1996, the world price of wheat and corn—the two leading grains in terms of quantity produced—again more than doubled.[29]

As of 1997, the world consumes 5 million tons of grain a day. Thus, rebuilding the grain stocks from the 57 days of carryover for 1997 to 70 days will require an increase in production over consumption of 65 million tons—a gain that would have been easy to achieve during the 1980s, when large parts of U.S. cropland were held out of production, but one that will be much more difficult in the 1990s.[30]

The long-term decline in the price of wheat, the world's leading food staple, that has been under way since mid-century may have bottomed out during the 1990s. (See Figure 5.) After dropping to a recent low of $3.97 per bushel in 1993, the price increased in each of the next three years,

FIGURE 4

World Grain Carryover Stocks, as Days of Consumption, 1961–97

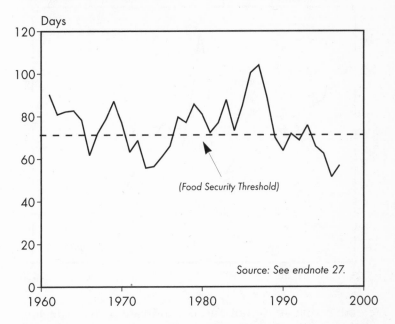

(Food Security Threshold)

Source: See endnote 27.

reaching $5.54 per bushel in 1996, a rise of 39 percent. While future year-to-year price changes will sometimes be down, as may be the case in 1997, this analysis indicates that the long-term trend is likely to be up.[31]

In some countries that are not completely integrated into the global food economy, prices have risen even faster. For example, the price of wheat at the beginning of 1997 within China was 49 percent above the world market price. In the *National Conditions Report No. 5*, published by the Chinese Academy of Sciences, this higher price for wheat and, to a lesser extent, for other grains, was acknowledged with obvious concern.[32]

Another factor affecting future world food security is the substantial share of current food production that is based on the unsustainable use of land and water. For example, a small fraction of the world's cropland is so highly

World Wheat Price, 1950–96

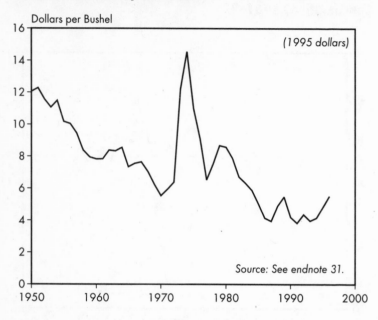

erodible that it cannot sustain cultivation over the long term. Eventually it will be abandoned. An even larger share of the world's irrigated agriculture may be based on the unsustainable use of water. As aquifers are depleted, many countries face a cutback in irrigation water supplies.

As a result of this growing imbalance, the politics of surpluses that dominated the world food economy during the half-century following World War II is being replaced by a politics of scarcity. The traditional question of how a handful of grain-exporting countries could gain access to import markets is being replaced by concern about how importing countries can be assured of unrestricted access to exporters' grain supplies at a time of scarcity and rising food prices.

Land and Water Scarcity

As the world's population, now approaching 5.8 billion, continues to expand by 80 million a year, both the area of cropland and the amount of irrigation water per person are shrinking, threatening to drop below the level needed to provide minimal levels of food security.[33]

Over time, farmers have used ingenious methods to expand the area used to produce crops. These included irrigation, terracing, drainage, fallowing, and even, for the Dutch, reclaiming land from the sea. Terracing let farmers cultivate steeply sloping land on a sustainable basis, quite literally enabling them to farm the mountains as well as the plains. Drainage of wetlands opened fertile bottomlands for cultivation. Alternate-year fallowing to accumulate moisture helped farmers extend cropping into semiarid regions.

By mid-century, the frontiers of agricultural settlement had largely disappeared, contributing to a dramatic slow-down in the growth in area planted to grain. Between 1950 and 1981, the grain area increased from 587 million to 732 million hectares, a gain of nearly 25 percent. After reaching a record high in 1981, the area in grain declined, dropping to 683 million hectares in 1993. It has turned upward since then, increasing to 696 million hectares in 1996 as idled cropland was returned to production and as record grain prices in the spring of 1996 led farmers to shift land out of soybeans and other oilseeds.[34]

Changes in the grainland area are the net effect of various trends that either add to or subtract from the cropland base. Among these are the loss of cropland to erosion and other forms of degradation and the conversion of cropland to nonfarm uses, such as residential development, industrial development, highway construction, and golf courses. In recent decades, some of the world's grainland has also been shifted to oilseeds, importantly soybeans. On the other side of the balance sheet, increasing the grainland area are the plowing of grassland, the clearing of forestland, the extension of agriculture into arid areas as a result of irrigation expansion, and the drainage of wetlands.

Part of the expansion from 1950 until roughly 1980 was on land that was subject to severe soil erosion by wind or water, much of it in the former Soviet Union. The peak Soviet grain area of 123 million hectares in 1977 shrank to 89 million hectares in 1996, declining almost every year as falling productivity forced the abandonment of marginal, often heavily eroded land.[35]

In the United States, a more formal effort was made to rescue highly erodible land that was plowed in response to the high grain prices of the mid-1970s. In 1985, Congress—with the strong support of environmental groups—passed the Conservation Reserve Program, an initiative designed to retire much of this land by paying farmers to return it to grass before it became wasteland. By 1990, some 14 million hectares of this vulnerable land had been set aside under long-term contracts.[36]

Few countries have attempted to assess carefully the effect of soil erosion on future land productivity. One that has is Kazakstan. After reaching 25 million hectares in the mid-1980s, the area sown to grain there began to decline, shrinking to 18.6 million hectares in 1995 as marginal land was abandoned. A study by the country's Institute of Soil Management sees this shrinkage continuing before stabilizing at 13 million hectares. The progressive effect of soil erosion, mostly from wind and other forms of land degradation in this region of low rainfall, has reduced yields on the marginal land areas to less than 500 kilograms per hectare, well below that in most African countries.[37]

The United States and Kazakstan are just two countries that have tried to measure soil erosion and assess its effect on the long-term productivity of land. If other governments were to undertake similar exercises, many would likely discover that they, too, will lose a share of their cropland. They could face a choice of converting eroding cropland to grassland, often its only sustainable use, or letting it erode until it becomes wasteland.

In addition to soil erosion, another leading source of cropland loss is industrialization, a trend that is strongest in countries already densely populated when rapid industrialization gets under way. The subsequent changes claim large areas of land for the construction of factories and warehouses, as does the evolution of an automobile-centered transportation system.

Indeed, one of the leading potential cropland claimants in Asia, particularly in China and India, is the automobile. In 1995, China had only 2 million cars—barely 1 percent as large as the U.S. fleet. An increase to 22 million cars by 2010, as now projected, would lead to land being paved for a national network of highways and roads and for streets, parking lots, and service stations on a scale that will inevitably take a toll on the country's scarce cropland.[38]

Few countries have assessed carefully the effect of soil erosion on future land productivity.

India, too, will be sacrificing cropland to the automobile, trading the prestige of car ownership by a few for the food security of the many. In 1996, Indian automobile output expanded by an estimated 26 percent, with further gains in prospect as the world's major automobile manufacturers flock to the country.[39]

Compounding the loss of grainland to nonfarm uses is the conversion of substantial areas to other crops, such as oilseeds, fruits, and vegetables, as industrialization progresses and incomes rise. From 1950 to 1996, the world's harvest of soybeans—which dominates oilseed production—climbed from 17 million to 133 million tons as demand for protein supplements for livestock and poultry feed and for cooking oil soared. With farmers unable to raise rapidly the yield per hectare of this crop, the land in soybeans increased from 14 million hectares in 1950 to 62 million hectares in 1995, with growth coming largely at the expense of grain, especially during the last two decades. (See Figure 6.)[40]

All these economic forces have been at work in Japan,

South Korea, and Taiwan, which have lost nearly half their grainland area since it peaked around 1960. As Asia industrializes, the construction of factories, roads, parking lots, and new cities is eating into the remaining productive cropland. In more affluent regions, land is also being claimed by shopping centers, tennis courts, golf courses, and private villas. In China's rapidly industrializing Guangdong Province, an estimated 40 golf courses have been built in the newly affluent Pearl River delta region alone. In 1995, concern about the effect on food production of this wholesale loss of cropland led the Guangdong Land Bureau to cancel the construction of all golf courses planned but not yet completed.[41]

China has experienced a particularly rapid loss of cropland in the southern coastal provinces, including Guangdong, where much of the rice crop is produced. Land now occupied by factories in southern China was just a few years ago producing two or three crops of rice per year. This is some of the most productive cropland not only in China but in the world. Other Asian countries, including India, Indonesia, Malaysia, Thailand, and Viet Nam, are also facing heavy losses as industrialization claims some of the region's best cropland.[42]

Despite frequent claims about vast opportunities for expanding the earth's cultivated area, the chances to do so at food prices that the world's poor can afford are in fact quite limited. With a doubling of grain prices, some marginal land, such as the cerrado (dry plain) in eastern Brazil, might be profitably cultivated. But this is unlikely to do little more than help meet rapidly growing local demand. Brazil, now the largest grain importer in the western hemisphere, is facing a population increase of some 40 million by 2030 and a widespread rise in affluence that is boosting consumption of livestock products. If it can become self-sufficient in grain, it will be doing well; it is unlikely to have much left over to export to densely populated countries such as Bangladesh, China, or Indonesia.[43]

There are still a few places in the world where additional land can be brought under the plow. In Argentina, for

World Soybean Area, 1950–96

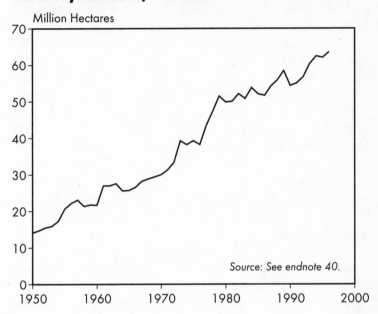

Source: See endnote 40.

example, some land now used for grazing can be converted to crop production, if properly managed to limit soil erosion. Although this is not a vast area, it could help expand domestic grain production and exports. Similarly, Indonesia has some potential for expanding production on its outer islands. Although most of the land there should be left in tropical rainforest, there are some areas that could sustain grain cultivation if properly managed.

As noted earlier, in 1996 the United States returned to production the limited area of cropland that was still idled under commodity programs, which have since been dismantled. In the fall of 1996, most of the 10 percent of the European Union's cropland that was idled under the Common Agricultural Policy was also brought back into production with the planting of wheat, barley, and other winter grain crops. The only U.S. cropland still idled is that in the Conservation Reserve Program. Roughly half of that

14 million hectares could be returned to production and farmed sustainably, adding annually perhaps 28 million tons of additional grain, enough to cover world population growth for one year.[44]

The world grain harvested area expanded from 1950 until it peaked in 1981, but the growth was quite slow compared with that of population. As a result, the grainland area per person has been declining steadily since mid-century, shrinking from 0.23 hectares in 1950 to 0.12 hectares in 1996. If grainland gains and losses continue to offset each other in the decades ahead, the area will remain stable at roughly 700 million hectares. But with population projected to grow at some 80 million a year over the next few decades, the amount of cropland available to produce grain will continue to decline, shrinking to 0.08 hectares per person in 2030. (See Figure 7.)[45]

In addition to land scarcity, more and more of the world's farmers are now facing water scarcity. The expanding demand for water is pushing beyond the sustainable yield of aquifers in many countries and is draining some of the world's major rivers dry before they reach the sea. As the demand for water for irrigation and for industrial and residential uses continues to expand, the competition between countryside and city for available water supplies intensifies. In some parts of the world, meeting growing urban needs is possible only by diverting water from irrigation.

One of the keys to the near tripling of the world grain harvest from 1950 to 1990 was a 2.5-fold expansion of irrigation, a development that extended agriculture into arid regions with little rainfall, intensified production in low-rainfall areas, and increased dry-season cropping in countries with monsoonal climates. It also accounts for part of the phenomenal growth in world fertilizer use since mid-century. Most of the world's rice and much of its wheat is produced on irrigated land.[46]

From the beginning of irrigation several thousand years ago until 1900, irrigated area expanded slowly, eventually covering some 40 million hectares. From 1900 to

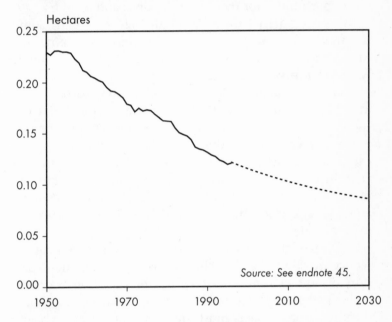

FIGURE 7

Grain Area Per Person, 1950–96, With Projections to 2030

Hectares

Source: See endnote 45.

1950, the pace picked up, and the total area more than doubled to 94 million hectares. But the big growth occurred from 1950 to 1994, when 155 million hectares were added, bringing the total to 249 million hectares.[47]

A key threshold was crossed in 1979. From 1950 until then, irrigation expanded faster than population, increasing the irrigated area per person by nearly one third. This was closely associated with the worldwide rise in grain production per person of one third. But since 1979, the growth in irrigation has fallen behind that of population, shrinking the irrigated area per person by some 7 percent. This trend, now well established, will undoubtedly continue as the demand for water presses ever more tightly against available supplies.[48]

The best conditions for irrigating with river water are found in Asia, which has some of the world's great rivers—

the Indus, the Ganges, the Chang Jiang (Yangtze), the Huang He (Yellow), and the Brahmaputra. These originate at high elevations and travel long distances, providing numerous opportunities for dams and the diversion of water into networks of gravity-fed canals and ditches. As a result, some two thirds of the world's irrigated area is in Asia. China and India lead the world, with 50 million and 48 million hectares of irrigated land respectively.[49]

In monsoonal climates, where the wet season is followed by several months of little or no rain, irrigation holds the key to cropping intensity. Where temperatures permit year-round cropping, as they often do in such climates, irrigation allows the production of two or even three crops a year. In China, rapid irrigation expansion helped farmers move from growing an average of 1.3 crops per hectare in 1950 to 1.5 crops by 1980, which is roughly where it remains today.[50]

During the 1990s, several trends are emerging to reduce irrigated area. Principal among these are the depletion of aquifers and the diversion of irrigation water to cities. Water tables are now falling in the major food-producing regions. This is most dramatic where irrigated agriculture depends on fossil water, such as in the Ogallala aquifer underlying the southern Great Plains of the United States and in Saudi Arabia.[51]

In the U.S. Great Plains, farmers from Nebraska south through Kansas, eastern Colorado, Oklahoma, and the Texas panhandle greatly expanded irrigation from mid-century through 1980 by tapping the vast Ogallala aquifer. Although in some locales this does receive a modest recharge from rainfall, most of the water in it was deposited there eons ago. Heavy reliance on the Ogallala is therefore ultimately unsustainable. In some of its more shallow southern reaches, it is already partly depleted. As a result, between 1982 and 1992 irrigated area in Texas shrank 11 percent, forcing farmers to return to traditional—and less productive—dryland farming. Irrigated area is also shrinking in Oklahoma, Kansas, and Colorado. The U.S. Department of Agriculture reports that 21 percent of U.S. irrigated land is watered by aquifer depletion.[52]

In India, water tables are falling in several states, including the Punjab—the country's breadbasket. The double cropping of high-yielding, early-maturing wheat and rice there has dramatically boosted the overall grain harvest since the mid-1960s, but unfortunately it has pushed water use beyond the sustainable yield of the underlying aquifer. Water tables are also falling in several other states, including parts of the semiarid state of Rajasthan in India's northwest. As this happens, cities and towns drill deeper wells. Meanwhile, villagers without the capital to deepen their own wells are left high and dry, forced to abandon irrigated agriculture.[53]

In China, which is trying to feed 1.2 billion increasingly affluent consumers, much of the northern part of the country is a water-deficit region, satisfying part of its needs by overpumping aquifers. Under Beijing, for example, the water table dropped from 5 meters below ground level in 1950 to more than 50 meters below in the 1990s.[54]

Professor Chen Yiyu, vice president of the Chinese Academy of Sciences, reports that under a large area of northern China the water table has fallen some 30 meters over the last two to three decades. He estimates that about 100 million people live in the affected area. At some point in the future, the aquifer will be depleted. Whether that is imminent or still some years away is not clear. But whenever it comes, it will reduce abruptly the supply of water for this population. Meeting residential and industrial needs for water may be possible only with a steep cutback in irrigation.[55]

The geographic region of the world most affected by water scarcity is North Africa and the Middle East. From Morocco in the west to Iran in the east, a majority of the countries in the region import half or more of their grain. Agriculture in country after country in the region, including Tunisia, Israel, and Iran, is dependent on overpumping of aquifers, something that by definition cannot be sustained indefinitely. When these aquifers are depleted, it will lead to cutbacks in irrigation and in food production, leaving the region even more dependent on the outside world for food supplies.

Perhaps the most dramatic irrigation cutback to date has occurred in Saudi Arabia, an arid country where agriculture depends heavily on irrigation. After the oil export embargo in the early 1970s, the Saudis realized they would be similarly vulnerable to a grain export embargo. To eliminate this threat, they decided to develop a system of irrigated agriculture that would draw on a fossil aquifer. To make the exploitation of this aquifer profitable, the Saudis adopted a price support for wheat of $24 a bushel, more than six times the world market price. As a result of this and other measures, grain production in Saudi Arabia increased from 260,000 tons in 1980 to 5 million tons in 1994. At this point, however, both the aquifer and the Saudi treasury were being depleted, leading to a heavy cut in the subsidies. Between 1994 and 1996, Saudi grain production dropped by 62 percent. (See Figure 8.)[56]

The Saudis are among the first to experience abrupt cutbacks in irrigation, but they will not be the last. Although few reductions will be as abrupt, cutbacks in many states or provinces are either under way or imminent in the United States, India, and China, and in several countries in North Africa and the Middle East.

The growing demand for water is putting excessive pressure on rivers as well as aquifers. The planet's great rivers are perpetually renewing, but in more populated regions, rivers have been dammed, diverted, and tapped until often there is little water left to continue on its way. In fact, many rivers now run dry before they reach the ocean.

China's great Huang He (Yellow River), which first failed to reach the sea in 1972, now runs dry each year and for progressively longer periods. In the late spring of 1996, it completely disappeared before it reached Shandong Province, the last one it travels through en route to the Yellow Sea. For the farmers of Shandong, who produce one fifth of China's wheat and one seventh of its corn and who

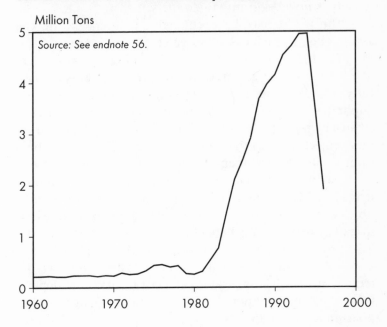

FIGURE 8

Saudi Arabia Grain Production, 1960–96

Million Tons

Source: See endnote 56.

depend on the river for half their irrigation water, this was not good news.[57]

At the same time, the major river in southwestern United States—the Colorado—now disappears into the Arizona desert, rarely reaching the Gulf of California. And in central Asia, the Amu Dar'ya is drained dry by Turkmen and Uzbek cotton farmers before it reaches the Aral Sea, thus contributing not only to the sea's gradual disappearance but also to the collapse of the 44,000 ton-per-year fishery it once supported.[58]

As countries or regions begin to press against the limits of water supplies, the competition between the cities and the countryside intensifies. The cities almost always win. As water is pulled away from agriculture, production often drops, forcing the country to import grain. Importing a ton of grain is, in effect, importing a thousand tons of water. For countries with water shortages, importing grain is the most efficient way to import water. Just as land scarcity has shaped international grain trade patterns historically, water scarcity is now beginning to do the same.[59]

The world may have entered a new era during the 1990s, one in which overall irrigated area no longer increases. A few irrigation projects are still coming on stream here and there, including a large one in Turkey that is systematically tapping the remaining unused potential of the Euphrates River. Viet Nam is planning to expand its irrigated area by tapping the waters of the Mekong. But gains from new projects such as these may be offset by losses elsewhere from aquifer depletion and the diversion of water to cities.[60]

David Seckler, Director General of the International Irrigation Management Institute, believes the losses may now be exceeding the gains, leading to a shrinkage of world irrigated area. If this is happening, as seems likely, then the irrigation water supply per person—which has declined slowly for some years—will fall even faster. Arresting the reduction in irrigation water per person may now depend more on stabilizing population than on anything else that policymakers can do.[61]

If the world irrigated area does manage to hold steady at 250 million hectares in the decades ahead, the irrigated area per person still will shrink steadily, making it much more difficult to increase grain production per person. If population grows as projected, the irrigated area per person will decline from 0.043 hectares per person in 1997 to 0.030 hectares per person in 2030, a decline of more than 30 percent. (See Figure 9.)[62]

The bottom line is that the world's farmers face a steady shrinkage in both grainland and irrigation water per person. As cropland and irrigation water become ever more scarce, prices of both are likely to rise, pushing grain prices upward.

Aquifer depletion and the future cutbacks in water supplies that will eventually follow may pose a far greater threat to economic progress than most people realize. If aquifer depletion were simply a matter of a few isolated instances, it

FIGURE 9

World Irrigated Area Per Person, 1950–95, With Projections to 2030

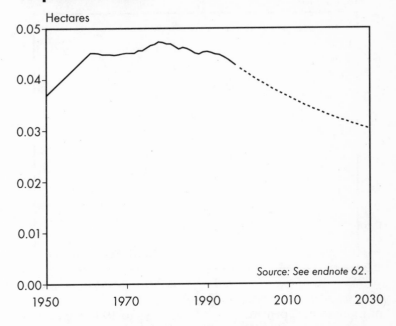

Source: See endnote 62.

would be one thing, but it is now in evidence in scores of countries. Among those suffering from extensive aquifer depletion are China, India, and the United States—the three countries that collectively account for about half of the world grain harvest.[63]

There is a tendency in public discourse to talk about the water problem and the food problem as though they are independent. But with some 70 percent of all the water that is pumped from underground or diverted from rivers used for irrigation (20 percent is used by industry and 10 percent for residential purposes), the water problem and the food problem are in large measure the same. Given the fundamental role of water in food production, it is only a matter of time until water scarcity translates into food scarcity.[64]

Even as land becomes scarce, the ability to raise land productivity is weakening. The rise in grain yield per hectare

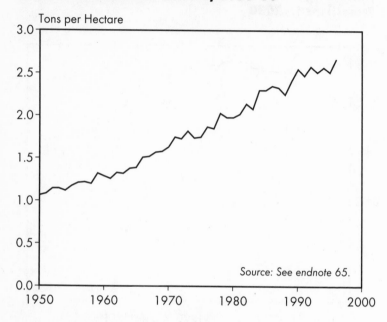

FIGURE 10

World Grain Yield Per Hectare, 1950–96

of more than 2 percent a year from 1950 to 1990 appears to have dropped to roughly 1 percent a year during the 1990s. (See Figure 10.) The central question now is whether scientists can help farmers restore the rapid rise in land productivity.[65]

A Century of Yield Takeoffs

The first recorded case in which a country's farmers achieved a sharp increase in output per unit of land—a "yield takeoff"—began more than a century ago in Japan. In 1878, Japanese rice farmers got an average of 1.4 tons of grain per hectare. By 1984, the average yield had more than tripled, to 4.7 tons. Since then, it has plateaued—fluctuating between 4.3 and 4.6 tons in all but three years. (See Figure 11.) Despite the fact that the government supports the price paid to its farmers for rice at six times the world level, thereby offering a powerful financial incentive to raise yields higher, and despite its ability to provide the best technology available, Japan has been unable to improve average rice yields for more than a decade.[66]

In the United States, the first yield takeoff came more than a half-century later, with wheat. During the nearly 80 years between the Civil War and World War II, U.S. wheat yields had fluctuated around 0.9 tons per hectare. As the war got under way and demand for U.S. grain rose as production was disrupted abroad, farmers began investing in higher-yielding seeds and in fertilizer. By 1983, wheat yields had climbed to 2.65 tons per hectare, nearly tripling the traditional level. Since then, however, there has been no further rise. Although the wheat yield takeoff in the United States began decades after that of rice in Japan, farmers in the two

FIGURE 11

Rice Yield for Japan (1878–1996) and Wheat Yield for United States (1866–1996)

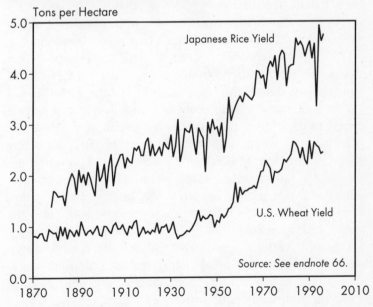

Source: See endnote 66.

countries appear to have "hit the wall" at about the same time. Experts have good reason to wonder whether this plateauing in two of the most agriculturally advanced countries signals a future leveling off in other countries, as farmers exhaust all known means of increasing yields.[67]

The 2.5-fold increase in world grain land productivity since mid-century has come from three sources: genetic advances, agronomic improvements, and some synergies between the two.

On the genetic front, the principal growth has come from redistributing the share of the plant's photosynthetic product (photosynthate) going to each of the various plant parts (leaves, stems, roots, and seeds) so that a much larger share goes to the seed—the part used for food. Scientists estimate that the originally domesticated wheats devoted roughly 20 percent of their photosynthate to the development of seeds; they were stalk-heavy and harvest-light. Through plant breeding, it has been possible to raise the share of photosynthate going into seed—the "harvest index"—in today's wheat, rice, and corn to more than 50 percent. Given the plant's basic requirements of an adequate root system, a strong stem, and sufficient leaves for photosynthesis, scientists believe the physiological limit is around 60 percent.[68]

One of the earliest gains in this area came when Japanese scientists incorporated a dwarf gene into rice and wheat plants during the late nineteenth century. Traditional varieties of these grasses were tall and thin because their ancestors growing in the wild needed to compete with other plants for sunlight. But once farmers began controlling weeds among the domesticated plants, there was no longer a need for tall varieties. As plant breeders shortened both wheat and rice plants, reducing the length of their straw, they also lowered the share of photosynthate going into the straw and increased that going into seed. L.T. Evans, a prominent Australian soil scientist and plant physiologist who has long studied cereal yield gains and potentials, notes that in the high-yielding dwarf wheats, "the gain in grain yield approximately equals the loss in straw weight."[69]

With corn, varieties grown in the tropics were reduced in height from an average of nearly three meters to less than two. But Don Duvick, for many years the director of research at the Pioneer Hybrid seed company, observes that with the hybrids used in the U.S. Corn Belt, the key to higher yields is the ability of varieties to "withstand the stress of higher plant densities while still making the same amount of grain per plant." One of the keys to growing more plants per hectare is to reorient the horizontally inclined leaves of traditional strains that droop somewhat, making them more upright and thereby reducing the amount of self-shading.[70]

Although plant breeders have greatly increased the share of the photosynthate going to the seed of various grains, they have not been able to fundamentally alter the basic process of photosynthesis itself. The amount produced by a given leaf area remains unchanged from that of the plant's wild ancestors.

Plant breeders have not been able to alter the basic process of photosynthesis.

On the agronomic front, the principal means of increasing land productivity have been to expand irrigation, use more fertilizer, and control diseases, insects, and weeds. All these tactics help plants reach more of their full genetic yield potential.

Fertilizer helps to ensure that plant growth will not be inhibited by any lack of nutrients. The tenfold rise in fertilizer use, from 14 million tons in 1950 to some 140 million in 1990, has been by far the most important agronomic source of higher land productivity since mid-century. (See Figure 12.) But in the 1990s, usage of fertilizer—like that of irrigation—has leveled off in many countries. U.S. farmers, after discovering that there are optimal levels beyond which further applications are not cost-effective, are using less fertilizer in the mid-1990s than they were in the early 1980s. This trend has been followed by similar developments in Western Europe and Japan.[71]

In the former Soviet Union, fertilizer use fell precipitously after subsidies were removed in 1988 and prices climbed to world market levels. After 1990, a combination of the breakup of the Soviet Union and the effort to convert from a planned to a market economy led to a severe economic depression, one even deeper than in the United States in the 1930s. The net effect of all this was a drop in fertilizer use of some four fifths in the former Soviet Union between 1988 and 1995. In 1995 and 1996, growth in fertilizer use in other parts of the world, particularly in countries such as China and India, and the leveling off of usage in the former Soviet Union restored growth in the world figure. This rise is likely to continue for some time into the future, with increases concentrated in countries such as India and Argentina that have adequate soil moisture but are using rather modest amounts of fertilizer.[72]

Other agronomic contributions to higher cropland productivity include the more timely planting of crops made possible by mechanization and higher plant populations per hectare, the latter applying particularly to corn. In temperate zones, there is typically a brief window of opportunity for seeding, usually measured in days, when optimum yields can be obtained. Yields decline with each day of delay.

Advances in plant breeding and agronomy often reinforce each other. The dwarfing of wheat and rice plants not only reduced the amount of photosynthate needed for straw, it increased the benefit of adding more fertilizer. For example, the traditional tall, thin-strawed wheat varieties grown in India could effectively use only about 40 kilograms of nitrogen per hectare. More than that made the plants grow heavier heads of grain, but these would often "lodge," or fall over (especially in storms), leading to crop losses. With the dwarf varieties, farmers could boost nitrogen applications to 120 kilograms per hectare or more, thus greatly increasing the yield but with little fear of lodging. This synergy between genetics and agronomics helps explain the doubling or tripling of yields achieved with the first generation of high-yielding wheats and rices—the heart of the Green Revolution.[73]

FIGURE 12

World Fertilizer Use, 1950–96

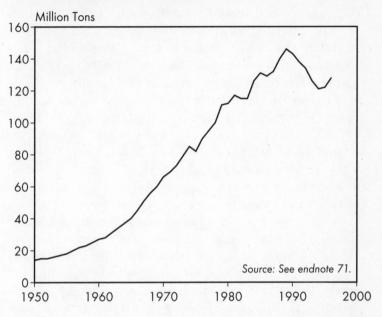

Source: See endnote 71.

With corn, the greater tolerance for crowding enabled growers to increase significantly the plant population—and hence the number of ears harvested—per hectare. At the same time, herbicides were being developed that would control weeds, eliminating the traditional need to plant corn rows far enough apart to permit mechanical cultivators to pass through the field early in the growing season. As a result of these two advances, plant populations have climbed. In Iowa, for example, corn plant densities have nearly tripled since 1930.[74]

For each of the three major grains—wheat, rice, and corn—the major worldwide gains in productivity took place between 1950 and 1990. Since 1990, gains have been much smaller, and the question now facing planners is just how much more can be expected.[75]

Raising Grain Yields

Yields of wheat, now humanity's principal food staple, vary enormously from one country to another. Kazakstan, the largest producer among the central Asian republics, produced only 0.6 tons per hectare in 1995, for example; France, the largest producer in Europe, produced more than 10 times as much that year—6.8 tons per hectare. It may be tempting to cite such disparities as evidence of potential for improvement in the lower-yielding countries, but this would be highly misleading. In fact, the prospect for raising yields further may actually be better in France than in Kazakstan. Rainfall is marginal for agriculture in Kazakstan, and with wind erosion of soil now widespread, Kazak soil scientists report that cropland fertility is falling.[76]

A look at the historical trends in such key wheat-producing countries as France, China, and the United States helps explain the potential for raising wheat yields throughout the world. In France, wheat yields have nearly quadrupled since mid-century, climbing from 1.8 tons per hectare in 1950 to 7.0 tons in 1996. (See Figure 13.) The United States, with a yield of just over 1 ton per hectare, ranked second after France in 1950. By 1983, farmers had pushed this above 2.6 tons per hectare. But as noted earlier, since then yields have been flat.[77]

The fallacy of thinking that low yields are a measure of the potential for improvement is further illustrated by a comparison of India and Australia. In 1950, both countries were getting the same yields from their wheat: about 0.9 tons per hectare. By 1995, India had nearly tripled its yield, to 2.5 tons. Australia has increased to only 1.7 tons. But the difference is not a reflection of the superior capabilities of Indian farmers. In fact, the Australians had to use great ingenuity and effort to achieve even the gains they got. The difference is that farmers in India, who irrigate much of their wheat, have good soil moisture, whereas those in Australia, who have to rely on sparse rainfall, do not. This also

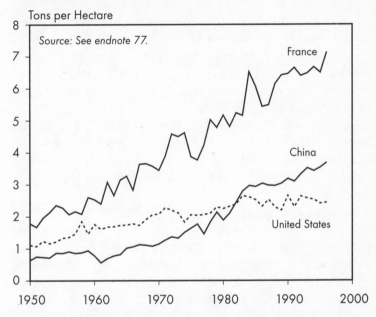

FIGURE 13

Wheat Yields in France, China, and the United States, 1950–96

Tons per Hectare

Source: See endnote 77.

France

China

United States

explains why Africa, a largely arid and semiarid continent, has not matched the yield gains of Asia. Lacking either abundant rainfall or irrigation to provide sufficient soil moisture, farmers cannot effectively use much fertilizer—and therefore cannot fully exploit the genetic potential of their crops.[78]

Grainland productivity is directly affected by soil moisture levels, latitude or day length, and solar intensity. In Table 1, the two countries with the highest wheat yields are in Western Europe. Both have good soil moisture and sufficiently mild climates that they can grow the higher-yielding winter wheats that benefit so much from the long summer days. The next two on the list—Egypt and Mexico—rely heavily on irrigation to achieve relatively high wheat yields. Indeed, in Egypt, where it rarely ever rains, wheat would not grow without irrigation. China, next on the list, relies on supplemental irrigation for much of its wheat crop.

Now that developing countries are collectively using more fertilizer than industrial countries and, with few exceptions, are using high-yielding varieties and other advanced technologies, ranking on the yield chart is determined largely by the environmental factors just mentioned—rainfall, day length, and solar intensity. When a country's wheat-growing practices do fall short of their potential, the yield can be improved rapidly until environmental limits are reached—and then no amount of money, ingenuity, or fertilizer can take it much further. The United States nearly tripled its wheat yield by 1983, for example, but even with all its access to technology, fertilizer, and agronomic knowledge, it has not been able to raise yields since then.

Raising wheat yields in China is becoming more difficult as aquifers are depleted, as the response to additional fertilizer diminishes, and as the country's fast-growing cities pull irrigation water away from agriculture. With the Huang He now running dry for several weeks each spring, and for progressively longer periods each year, some wheat farmers downstream will face shrinking irrigation water supplies.

In France and other major wheat-producing countries such as Germany and the United Kingdom, it took less than five years to go from 5 to 6 tons per hectare, but more than a decade to go from 6 to 7 tons per hectare. Almost everywhere that wheat is produced, in developing countries as well as highly mechanized ones, the historic rise in yields is slowing. Mexico, the site of the breeding program that produced the high-yielding dwarf wheats that came to be widely used in the Third World, has become the first developing country to "hit the wall" in efforts to raise wheat land productivity. Like the United States, Mexico has not seen any improvement in the past 13 years.[79]

Rice, to achieve its full yield potential, requires large quantities of water, either from the natural flooding that occurs in monsoonal climates or from irrigation. When farmers are forced to rely on monsoon flooding, they lack

TABLE 1

Wheat Yield Per Hectare in Key Producing Countries, 1995

Country	Yield[1]
	(tons)
United Kingdom	7.7
France	6.8
Egypt	5.6
Mexico	4.1
China	3.6
Poland	3.4
Ukraine	2.7
India	2.5
United States	2.5
Canada	2.3
Argentina	2.1
Pakistan	2.0
Australia	1.6
Russia	1.4
Kazakstan	0.6

[1]Yield for 1995 is calculated as the average of 1994-96 to minimize the effects of annual weather fluctuations.

Source: USDA, FAS, World Agricultural Production (Washington, DC: April 1997).

the water control needed to use fertilizer and pesticides effectively. Irrigation, then, is a primary determinant of rice yields. Countries with high rice yields irrigate a larger percentage of their riceland.

Japan, which has the highest yield among the major rice producers (see Table 2), irrigates 99 percent of its riceland—as does South Korea, which ranks a close second. In Bangladesh, where farmers harvest less than half as much rice per hectare as the Japanese or Koreans do, the irrigated share falls to 24 percent. Three fourths of the riceland in Bangladesh is subject to the whims of the monsoon.[80]

Rice is also affected by latitude, with yields rising as distance from the equator increases. In Japan, the northern-

TABLE 2

Rice Yield Per Hectare in Key Producing Countries, 1995

Country	Yield[1]
	(tons)
Japan	4.8
South Korea	4.7
China	4.2
Taiwan	4.1
Indonesia	2.9
Viet Nam	2.4
Philippines	1.9
India	1.9
Pakistan	1.8
Bangladesh	1.8

[1]Yield for 1995 is calculated as the average of 1994–96 to minimize the effects of annual weather fluctuations.

Source: USDA, FAS, *World Agricultural Production* (Washington, DC: April 1997).

most of the major rice-producing countries, days during the summer growing season can be several hours longer than in a country like Indonesia, which lies astride the equator.[81]

A third factor affecting rice yields is solar intensity. Asia, which produces 90 percent of the world's rice, is actually handicapped because the bulk of this crop is grown during the summer monsoon season, when extensive cloud cover reduces the amount of sunlight reaching fields. Although Japan's latitudinal advantage and full use of irrigation give it the highest output in Asia, yields are still one third below those in California, where there is an abundance of sunshine.[82]

The historical trends in rice yields in Japan, China, and India (see Figure 14) provide some insight into the longer term potential for raising world rice yields. As noted earlier, Japan tripled its per-hectare output over a century of genetic and agronomic improvements, plateauing in 1984.[83]

China made its improvements later, but it too appears to have tripled its rice yields. If the area planted to rice in

China is underestimated by 20-30 percent, as Chinese officials now believe is likely, then the yield per hectare of rice
is overstated and the actual yield may be closer to 3.5 tons
per hectare rather than the official 4.2. Nonetheless, if
China's rice yield is adjusted for the latitudinal handicap it
suffers relative to Japan, then its farmers may be approaching the same productivity ceiling as Japanese farmers face.
That conclusion is consistent with the observation that
China is using the full arsenal of yield-enhancing techniques: high-yielding varieties, nearly full irrigation, and the
world's highest consumption of fertilizer, which suggests
that it has little to gain by using much more.[84]

   In India, rice yields have doubled since mid-century,
from roughly 1 ton per hectare to 2 tons. Production in
India suffers from a lack of irrigation, and because it has
shorter days during the summer growing season than Japan,
it cannot realistically be expected to raise yields to anywhere
near those of Japan. Along with whatever potential for high-

FIGURE 14

Rice Yields in Japan, China, and India, 1950–96

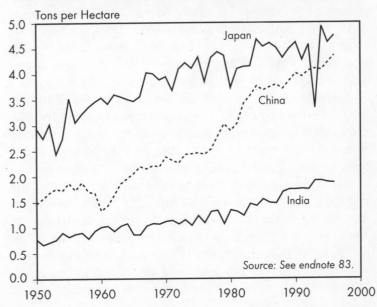

Source: See endnote 83.

er yields that may remain in India, the greatest promise appears to lie in Bangladesh, Viet Nam, and Myanmar (formerly Burma). But for the world as a whole, the unrealized opportunity to raise rice yields is shrinking, suggesting that future gains will be much slower.[85]

Perhaps the most promising source of higher rice yields is the new rice prototype being developed in the Philippines, which is expected to be available for commercial use sometime after the turn of the century. Dr. Gurdev Khush, the Indian scientist who heads the rice breeding project, believes it could raise rice yields in the tropical and subtropical regions, for which it is designed, by up to 20 percent. If it were to succeed in raising yields on two thirds of the world's riceland, this would boost the current world rice harvest of 350 million tons by 50 million tons, enough to cover the growth in demand for grain from world population growth for two years. Vitally important though this would be, it is a far cry from the doubling or tripling of yields that came with the first generation of high-yielding varieties.[86]

Corn yield, at just over 4 tons per hectare in 1995, is the highest of all the cereals—well above the 2.5 tons for wheat and rice. The prospect for raising that any further rests largely with the United States and China, the countries that account for two fifths and one fifth, respectively, of the world corn harvest. Both have been remarkably successful to date (see Table 3), more than quadrupling traditional levels.[87]

The U.S. corn yield of 7.9 tons per hectare in 1995 is the highest of any cereal in a major producing country. The rise in yields started there around 1940, the same time as for wheat and for essentially the same reasons: as grain prices rose, improved varieties became available and more fertilizer was applied. After fluctuating between 1.5 and 2 tons per hectare from the Civil War until the early 1940s, corn yields crossed the 2-ton threshold in 1942 for the first time. In 1957, 15 years later, they passed 3 tons per hectare. Then things really happened quickly. Five years later another ton was added. Another five years and another ton. And again. So from 1957 to 1972, U.S. farmers doubled corn yields from

TABLE 3

Corn Yield Per Hectare in Key Producing Countries, 1995

Country	Yield[1]
	(tons)
United States	7.9
China	4.9
Argentina	4.3
Brazil	2.5
South Africa	2.4
Mexico	2.2
Nigeria	1.8

[1]Yield for 1995 is calculated as the average of 1994–96 to minimize the effects of annual weather fluctuations.

Source: USDA, FAS, World Agricultural Production (Washington, DC: April 1997).

3 tons per hectare to 6 tons. (See Figure 15.)[88]

Then the rate of growth began to slow substantially. Going from 6 tons to 7 tons took 10 years. More recently, rising from 7 to 8 tons between 1982 and 1992, the rate of gain was only 1.6 percent a year. Despite these enormous gains, corn yields do not yet appear to be leveling off as wheat yields have.[89]

China, as a relative newcomer to modern corn production, has seen its yields rise rapidly. But they are not likely to reach U.S. levels, because unlike the United States, China does not reserve its best cropland for corn. Indeed, no other major corn-producing country has a region of deep, well-drained soils and near-ideal growing conditions comparable to the U.S. Midwest.

Argentina, where the 1995 corn yield was 4.3 tons per hectare, may have the largest unrealized potential for raising yields. Despite the high inherent fertility of the pampas, the country's past economic policies discouraged investment in agriculture, and little fertilizer was used. The recent elimination of heavy taxes on farm exports has set the stage for heavy investment in this sector. That, along with high world

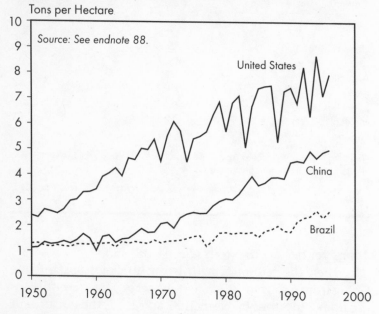

FIGURE 15

Corn Yields in the United States, China, and Brazil, 1950–96

Tons per Hectare

Source: See endnote 88.

United States

China

Brazil

1950   1960   1970   1980   1990   2000

corn prices, has already helped double fertilizer use in Argentina between 1994 and 1996.[90]

In Brazil, where the corn yield per hectare is only one third that of the United States, farmers are handicapped by a lack of the highly fertile, deep, well-drained soils on which corn thrives. A similar situation prevails in Mexico, where corn is grown largely by smallholders on marginal land in mountainous regions. These are typically hillside plots where low rainfall and thin soils—often heavily eroded—severely limit the yield potential.

Facing Biological Reality

For individual grains in individual countries, these historic trends show a sobering pattern. In every farming environment where yields have risen dramatically, there comes a time when the increase slows and either levels off or shows signs of doing so. It is equally revealing to look at the global trends. (Three-year averages are used here for the decennial or mid-decennial years in order to minimize the effects of weather variations; for example, the yield shown for 1990 is an average of the yield from 1989–91.)

From 1950 to 1990, the world's grain farmers raised the productivity of their land by an unprecedented 2.1 percent a year, but since 1990 there has been a dramatic loss of momentum. (See Table 4.) If the former Soviet Union is excluded from the global data for 1990 to 1995 because of the uncharacteristic drop in yields associated with economic reforms and the breakup of the country, the rate of yield gain rises from the 0.7 percent a year to 1.1 percent—roughly half that of the preceding 40 years. While the first half of the 1990s is too short a period to determine a new trend, it does provide cause for concern. In addition to the plateauing of wheat yields in the United States and Mexico cited earlier, yields in Canada and Egypt have shown no improvement so far in the 1990s.[91]

Global trends for the three major individual grains follow the pattern seen for grain as a whole. Rice production, which was modernized later than that of wheat and corn,

TABLE 4

Annual Change in World Grain Yields by Decade, 1950–95 (three-year average)

Year	Total Grain	Rice	Wheat	Corn	Other Grains
			(percent)		
1950–60	2.0	1.4	1.7	2.6	
1960–70	2.5	2.1	2.9	2.4	2.3
1970–80	1.9	1.7	2.1	2.7	0.4
1980–90	2.2	2.4	2.9	1.3	1.7
1990–95	0.7	1.0	0.1	1.7	−0.8

Source: USDA, "World Grain Database," unpublished printout, 1996; USDA, Production, Supply, and Distribution, electronic database, updated February 1997; USDA, FAS, World Agricultural Production (1997).

achieved an annual increase in productivity of 2.1 percent between 1960 and 1990 but has dropped to 1.0 percent since 1990. Wheat yields grew between 1960 and 1990 at an average of 2.6 percent a year, then slowed to 0.1 percent during the 1990s. (If the former Soviet Union, a major wheat producer, is excluded from the global trend after 1990, the figure is 1.0 percent.) Corn productivity rose on average 2.6 percent from 1950 to 1980, then fell to 1.3 percent in the 1980s. The rise in corn yields accelerated slightly during the first half of the 1990s, reaching 1.7 percent a year, largely because of a belated surge in yields in China and Brazil.[92]

With the slower rise in grainland productivity thus far during the 1990s, the obvious next question is whether the momentum can be regained through biotechnology. Yet progress is not promising there either. After 20 years of research, biotechnologists have not yet produced a single, high-yielding variety of wheat, rice, or corn. Why haven't some of the leading seed companies put biotechnologists to work developing a second generation of varieties that would again double or triple yields?

The answer, according to plant scientists, is that plant breeders using traditional techniques have largely exploited the genetic potential for increasing the share of photosynthate that goes into seed. Once this is pushed to its limit, the remaining options tend to be relatively small, clustering around efforts to raise the plant's tolerance of various stresses, such as drought or soil salinity. The one major option left to scientists is to increase the efficiency of the process of photosynthesis itself—something that has thus far remained beyond their reach.

When genetic yield potential is close to the physiological limit, further advances rely on the expanded use of basic inputs such as the fertilizer and irrigation needed to realize the plant's full genetic potential, or on the fine-tuning of other agronomic practices, such as the use of optimum planting densities or more effective pest controls. Beyond this, there will eventually come a point in each country, with each grain, when farmers will not be able to sustain the rise in yields.

U.S. Department of Agriculture plant scientist Thomas R. Sinclair observes that advances in plant physiology let scientists quantify crop yield potentials quite precisely. He notes that "except for a few options, which allow small increases in the yield ceiling, the physiological limit to crop yields may well have been reached under experimental conditions." This means that for farmers who are using the highest yielding varieties that plant breeders can provide, along with the agronomic inputs and practices needed to realize their genetic potential, there may be few options left to raise land productivity.[93]

Viewed broadly, an S-shaped growth curve begins to emerge for the historical rise in world grainland productivity. Throughout most human history, land productivity was static. Then beginning around 1880, Japan began to raise its rice yield per hectare in a steady, sustained fashion. By the mid-1950s, nearly all the industrial countries were expanding their grain harvest by raising grainland productivity. And by 1970, they had been joined by nearly all the leading grain producers in the developing world.[94]

Biotechnologists have not yet produced a single high-yielding variety of wheat, rice, or corn.

From 1970 to 1985, yields rose steadily in virtually all the grain-producing countries of any size. Then this unique period came to an end, as wheat yields in the United States and Mexico and rice yields in Japan leveled off. Eventually the rise in grain yields will level off everywhere, but exactly when this will occur in each country is difficult to anticipate. If more countries "hit the wall" in the years immediately ahead, as now seems likely, it will further slow the rise in world grainland productivity, dropping it well below growth in the world demand for grain.[95]

Except for the general warning by biologists that grain yields would eventually plateau, no specific warnings were heard in the early 1980s that the long rise of rice yields in

Japan or of wheat yields in the United States or Mexico were about to level off. Nor is anyone likely to anticipate precisely when, for example, wheat yields will level off in China, though this could occur at any time. A review of the last half-century's experience in raising yields does, however, offer certain generalizations.

One, the slower rise in grain yields since 1990 is not the result of something peculiar to individual grains or individual countries. It reflects a systemic difficulty in sustaining the gains that characterized the preceding four decades.

Two, every country that initiated a yield takeoff was able to sustain it for at least a few decades.

Three, most countries that have achieved a yield takeoff have managed at least to double if not triple or even quadruple traditional grain yields. Among those that have quadrupled such levels are the United States and China with corn; France, the United Kingdom, and Mexico with wheat; and China with rice.

Four, once plant breeders have essentially exhausted the possibilities for raising the genetic yield potential and once farmers are using the most advanced agronomic practices, including irrigation, the yield potential for any particular grain in a given country is determined largely by the physical environment of the country—mainly by soil moisture, but also by temperature, day length, and solar intensity. These factors are fundamentally unalterable.

Five, all countries are drawing on a common backlog of unused agricultural technology that is gradually diminishing and, for some crops in some countries—such as wheat in the United States and rice in Japan—that has largely disappeared, at least for the time being.

Six, as a general matter, the more recently a country has launched a yield takeoff, the faster its yields rise and the shorter the interval between yield takeoff and leveling off.

Seven, despite the slower rise in yields worldwide in recent years and the plateauing of yields in a few countries, many opportunities still exist for raising grainland productivity in most countries. These are most promising in coun-

tries where there is room for improvement in economic policies affecting agriculture. Although most governments sub-
sidize agriculture, some still have economic policies that dis-
courage investment in this sector. In these cases, the key to
realizing the full genetic yield potential of crops is the
restructuring of economic policies, as is happening now in
Argentina.

Even with a concerted worldwide effort to increase
grain yields, the rise during the last half of this decade could
slow still further, dropping below 1 percent a year—far below
the 2.1 percent that sustained the world from 1950 to 1990.[96]

The Emerging Politics of Scarcity

The slower rise in world grainland productivity during the
1990s may mark the transition from a half-century dominated by food surpluses to a future that will be dominated
by food scarcity. Among other things, this means the politics of surpluses will be replaced by a politics of scarcity, a
time when the issue will be not access to markets but access
to supplies. Will exporting countries be willing to guarantee
access to their grain supplies even in times of soaring grain
prices?

The vulnerability of grain importers is underlined by
their dependence for nearly half of their imports on the
United States, which controls a larger share of grain exports
than Saudi Arabia does of oil. This is inherently risky
because the U.S. grain harvest, largely rainfed, varies widely
from year to year, depending on temperature and rainfall. As
carbon dioxide levels have climbed and as temperatures
have risen over the last two decades or so, the U.S. grain
yield per hectare has become more volatile than it was during the 1950s and 1960s. Whether this is a consequence of
climate change and whether the yield swings will become
even wider if temperatures continue to rise, no one can say
for sure. But we do know that the record summer tempera-

tures in some recent years have dramatically reduced grain harvests in the country that supplies the world's grain-deficit countries with half of their imports.[97]

Farmers who have always had to cope with the vagaries of weather may now have to deal with climate change. The 13 warmest years since recordkeeping began in 1866 have all occurred since 1979. The four warmest years have come during the 1990s, with 1995 topping the list. Unfortunately for farmers and consumers, heat waves like those that shrank harvests in 1995 across the United States, Canada, several European countries, the Ukraine, and Russia could become even more frequent and intense if atmospheric carbon dioxide levels continue to build.[98]

Three times in the last nine years, the U.S. grain harvest has been reduced 17 percent or more by weather. When the grain yield per hectare was lowered in 1988 by 22 percent from the year before (see Figure 16), grain production dropped below consumption. Fortunately, the United States had vast grain stocks at the time and could satisfy the needs of importing countries by exporting some of them. In the event of a similar shortfall in the late 1990s, when grain stocks are at near-record lows, this will not be possible.[99]

After the summer of 1988, we know that severe heat and drought can reduce the U.S. grain harvest below domestic consumption, thus eliminating the exportable surplus. With world grain stocks now severely depleted, such knowledge should be of concern to food-importing countries everywhere.

In 1994, grain prices started to rise in China, climbing by nearly 60 percent as demand expanded faster than production. In an effort to check a price rise that was potentially politically destabilizing, China turned to the outside world for massive imports of grain, which in turn triggered an increase in world grain prices. As this happened, exporting countries were tempted to impose restrictions or even outright embargoes in order to control food prices at home.[100]

In the spring of 1995, for example, Viet Nam embargoed rice exports for some months simply because so much

THE EMERGING POLITICS OF SCARCITY

FIGURE 16

U.S. Grain Yield Per Hectare, 1950–96

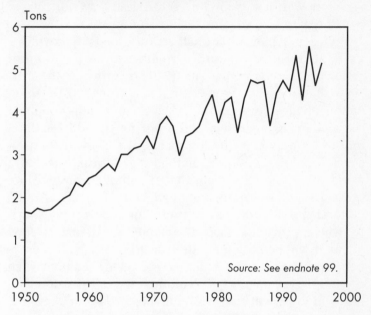

Source: See endnote 99.

of this staple had moved across its northern border into China, where rice prices were much higher, that it created potentially unmanageable inflationary pressures. In December 1995, the European Union, which ranks third as a grain exporter after the United States and Canada, imposed an export tax on wheat of $32 a ton in order to discourage exports and dampen the rise in bread prices within Europe. In January 1996 it did the same thing for barley, its principal feedgrain, because barley prices had nearly doubled, driving up prices of livestock products.[101]

Only when an exceptional 1997 world grain harvest was in prospect and grain prices dropped did the EU remove the export tax. But in April 1997, when wheat prices were again on the rise, officials in Brussels once more levied an export tax on wheat in order to prevent rises in bread prices within Europe. Whenever this happens, the EU in effect creates a two-price system for grain in the world: one within

Europe and another, much higher, outside it, where the world's low-income populations live. This is an early example of how rising grain prices can lead governments to restrict exports, putting importing countries at risk.[102]

Over much of the last half-century, food aid provided a safety net for needy countries, whether it was the war-torn nations of Europe in the late 1940s or Africa in the mid-1990s. But from fiscal year 1993 to fiscal year 1996, the international budget for food aid has been cut in half—dropping the amount of grain available from roughly 15.2 million tons to 7.6 million. With donor countries facing fiscal stringencies, political support for food aid is weakening. In a world of surpluses, the opportunity to simultaneously reduce excessive supplies and provide food assistance had a strong political appeal in donor countries. But in a world of scarcity, where providing food aid could raise domestic food prices, it will become more difficult to garner political support for such assistance. And this is occurring at a time when the U.S. Department of Agriculture estimates that food aid needs in 2005 will rise to 27 million tons—four times the amount available in 1996.[103]

In this new world of scarcity, countries that depend on imports for a large share of grain, mostly for food, are at risk. The countries of East Asia, such as Japan, South Korea, and Taiwan, that import at least 70 percent of their grain supplies are particularly vulnerable, though each does at least try to maintain self-sufficiency in the production of rice, the principal food staple. Also at risk are countries such as Algeria, Egypt, Iran, and Saudi Arabia, which import one third to two thirds of their grain.[104]

National security in this new era dictates that governments devise agricultural and population policies that permit them to avoid excessive dependence on imported food. The assumptions underlying population, agricultural, and trade policies during an age of surpluses need to be reassessed as the world moves into an age of scarcity. Despite the fashionable trend toward globalization, only the government of a country can assume responsibility for the food security of its people.

At the root of these difficult problems is population growth. Many countries with grain deficits at present are expected to have far larger deficits by 2030. In the Middle East, for example, the 1995 population of 215 million is projected to reach 443 million by 2030, forcing this water-limited region to depend on imports for most of its grain. The population of the northern tier of countries in Africa—from Morocco through Egypt, an area already facing acute water scarcity—is projected to grow from 137 million in 1995 to 234 million by 2030. Algeria, Israel, Jordan, Kuwait, Lebanon, Libya, Saudi Arabia, and Tunisia already import half or more of their grain.[105]

In a world of scarcity, it will become more difficult to garner political support for food aid.

The projected growth in population in sub-Saharan Africa is even more staggering, going from 588 million in 1995 to 1.37 billion in 2030. With thin soils and a limited potential for irrigation development, Africa seems destined to become a massive importer of grain—assuming that countries in the region can compete for what are likely to be scarce supplies.[106]

To the east, Asia's imports, growing by leaps and bounds, will continue to increase. China, already turning to the outside world for massive quantities of grain, may need to import some 200 million tons by 2030, an amount equal to current world exports.[107]

India's population, likely to pass 1 billion in late 1999, is projected to hit 1.4 billion in 2030. Already facing widespread groundwater depletion, it will likely be importing heavily. Pakistan, also now pushing against the limits of its water resources, is projected to increase its population from 126 million in 1995 to 224 million in 2030.[108]

As Mexico, with a 1995 population of 94 million, moves to 150 million in the year 2030, its current grain deficit is projected to be much larger—again because it is running into the limits of water supplies. Brazil, a country with one of the poorest agricultural land endowments of any major country and already the largest grain importer in the western hemisphere, is facing an increase from 161 million people in 1995 to 202 million in 2030.[109]

Many countries sense that they will need to import more grain, and all seem to assume that the United States will be able to cover their needs. But with little new land left to plow in the United States, this may not be easy. If the rise in U.S. land productivity continues to slow, dropping below population growth, expansion of exports will be more difficult in the future. At the same time, the export potential of both Canada and Australia is severely limited by rainfall. Argentina might be able to double its annual exports of 12 million tons if it plows enough of its grassland, but cropping has already expanded onto highly erodible land. Even a doubling of Argentinean exports would cover projected world population growth for only five months.[110]

With the global demand for grain beginning to outrun supplies, this analysis indicates that real grain prices (after adjusting for inflation) will rise in the years ahead—reversing the historical trend of declining real prices that was so strong through the early 1990s. This challenges projections done by the World Bank and the U.N. Food and Agriculture Organization of continuing surpluses and declining real grain prices through the year 2010. The government of Japan, on the other hand, has done a set of global projections that indicates that wheat and rice prices could double by 2010—an assessment much more consistent with the prospect outlined here.[111]

A doubling of grain prices, were it to occur, would impoverish more people in a shorter period of time than any event in history. Instead of reducing the number of malnourished people from 800 million to 400 million by 2010, as promised at the World Food Summit in Rome in late 1996, the number of hungry would mushroom, dashing confidence in the capacity of our political institutions to deal with this most pressing issue.[112]

As the world moves into an era of food scarcity, the international safety net that has existed during the half-century since World War II is disappearing. With the dismantling of U.S. farm commodity programs, there is obviously no cropland idled under these programs. World grain carryover stocks, meanwhile, have dropped below 60 days of consumption—little more than pipeline supplies. Even with idled cropland back in use in 1996 and 1997, the world was unable to rebuild depleted grain stocks. With little likelihood of a 1997 harvest that will permit rebuilding of carryover stocks in 1998, the world will have suffered through three years of stocks below 60 days of consumption, a level well below the 70-day minimum needed to cushion even one poor harvest.[113]

If prices rise in the future, how will they affect production? Historically, when grain prices climbed, production responded strongly. Farmers would bring more land under the plow. Unfortunately, the experience of the last several decades suggests that the opportunities for expanding the cropland area are limited.

In the past, farmers also responded to higher grain prices by investing more in developing water resources. When grain prices doubled in the 1970s, investment in irrigation wells climbed, helping to expand production. But in the late 1990s, investment in more irrigation wells in most food-producing regions of the world will simply accelerate the depletion of aquifers. In this situation it is not the investment in irrigation wells but the sustainable yield of aquifers that determines the availability of irrigation water. Simply stated, the traditional economic determinant of irrigation water supplies is being replaced by an environmental determinant.

Similarly, in the 1970s farmers could substantially expand fertilizer use as grain prices rose. But in much of the world, applying additional fertilizer during the 1990s will have little effect on yields. Again, an environmental constraint—the physiological capacity of existing crop varieties to absorb fertilizer—is replacing an economic constraint, the availability of credit with which farmers could buy fertilizer.

Historically, the principal determinant of the size of the fish catch was the investment in fishing capacity: spending more on fishing trawlers increased the harvest. But with fisheries being pushed to their sustainable-yield limits, this approach just leads to stock depletion and a decline in catch. Whereas in the past, the size of the fish catch was fixed largely by the amount of capital invested in fishing trawlers, today it is the sustainable yield of fisheries that governs the size of the catch.

This is not to say there will be no production response to higher grain prices in the 1990s. There will be. But it will be muted compared with earlier responses simply because some key economic determinants of production levels are being eclipsed by environmental determinants. And sometimes the response will simply be different. Instead of investing in more wells, for example, a farmer may invest in more-efficient irrigation equipment.

On the demand side, there will also be adjustments in times of scarcity. The supply and demand of grain always balance in the marketplace, but at much higher price levels. The key question is, What will be the social and economic effects of these price rises?

Even a doubling of world grain prices is not likely to have a major direct affect on the world's affluent. First, the affluent spend a relatively small percentage of their income on food. If necessary, this share could be expanded. And second, a good deal of the food expenditure in affluent societies is not for the original agricultural commodities themselves but for the processing. For example, in the United States a loaf a bread costing $1 may contain only 10¢ worth of wheat. A doubling of the price of wheat would add 10¢ to the price of the loaf. With poultry, it is unlikely that more than 30 percent of U.S. consumer expenditure is accounted for by the price of grain used to produce the poultry. Higher food prices at the supermarket checkout counter would be annoying, but they would not be life-threatening.[114]

For the 1.3 billion people in the world who live on a

dollar a day or less, however, a doubling in grain prices would be life-threatening. To begin with, people at this income level probably spend 70 percent or more of their income for food. They cannot afford processed foods. They buy wheat as wheat and mill it into flour themselves. Or they buy rice and cook it directly.[115]

The heads of households who could no longer buy enough food to keep their families alive would hold their governments responsible. They would almost certainly take to the streets, creating an unprecedented political instability in Third World cities, one that could affect the functioning of the economy. It could affect the earnings of multinational corporations, the performance of stock markets, the earnings of pension funds, and the stability of the international monetary system itself.

It is these indirect effects of food scarcity on the international economic system that will most likely affect the world's affluent. In an increasingly integrated global economy, the problem posed for the poor by rising food prices becomes everyone's problem. Bread riots in Egypt could affect the political stability of the Middle East. Rice riots in Indonesia could affect political stability in an oil-exporting country. Food prices spiraling out of control in Mexico could drive untold numbers across the border into the United States.

An Unprecedented Challenge

It is not easy to find the words to describe the scale of the effort needed to secure an adequate food supply for the next generation, since it depends on reversing the deeply ingrained trends of global environmental deterioration cited at the beginning of this paper. The words massive, mammoth, and enormous come to mind. But they do not fully convey the scale or urgency of the effort needed. In searching for historical analogies, only World War II comes close. But even that massive mobilization does not match the many dimensions of the effort outlined here.

Making sure that the next generation has enough food is no longer merely an agricultural matter. Historically, food security was the responsibility of the Ministry of Agriculture. Food scarcity often could be alleviated simply by fine-tuning farm policies and investing more in agriculture. Now achieving an acceptable balance between food and people depends as much on family planners as on farmers. Decisions made in the ministries of energy that will affect future climate stability may have as much effect on the food security of the next generation as those made in agricultural ministries.

The two most difficult components of the effort to secure future food supplies and build an environmentally sustainable economy are stabilizing population and climate. The former depends on a revolution in human reproductive behavior; the latter, on a restructuring of the global energy economy. Either would thoroughly challenge a single generation, but our generation must attempt both simultaneously. In addition, building an environmentally sustainable economy depends on reversing deforestation, arresting the loss of plant and animal species, and stabilizing fisheries, aquifers, and soils.

In a world where both the seafood catch and the grain harvest per person are declining, it may be time to reassess population policy. For example, some governments, facing a deterioration in their food situation, may have to ask if couples are morally justified in having more than two children, the number needed to replace themselves.

The world has taken one small step in the right direction with the stabilization of population in some 32 countries—all of them except Japan in Europe. These countries, home to some 14 percent of the world's people, clearly demonstrate that population stabilization is possible.[116]

But if family planners are to assume the principal responsibility for balancing food and people, they need more resources. The most urgent need is getting family planning services to the 120 million women, mostly in the Third World, who want to limit family size but lack access to the services needed to do so. At the same time, there is a need to invest heavily in the education of young females throughout the Third World. The social trend that correlates most closely with a shift to smaller families is the educational level of females. Simply stated, the more education women have, the fewer children they have.[117]

Stabilizing climate means reducing carbon emissions and, hence, fossil fuel burning—not an easy undertaking given that 85 percent of all commercial energy comes from fossil fuels. The outline of the solar/hydrogen economy that is likely to replace the fossil-fuel-based economy of today is beginning to emerge. Both the technology and the economics of harnessing solar and wind energy on a massive scale are beginning to fall into place. Although still minute in size compared with fossil fuel use, wind-generated electricity is expanding by more than 20 percent a year and the use of solar cells is expanding almost as fast.[118]

The second major opportunity for reducing carbon emissions is raising the efficiency of energy use. The impressive gains in boosting energy efficiency following the oil price shocks of the 1970s have waned in recent years. Adoption of a carbon tax (offset by a reduction in income taxes) that even partly reflected the costs of air pollution, acid rain, and climate disruption from burning fossil fuels would accelerate investment in solar and wind energy as well as in energy efficiency.

The replacement of surpluses with scarcity obviously argues for a far heavier investment of both private and public funds in agriculture itself. This includes investments in agricultural research, cropland protection, soil conservation, water efficiency, and the reduction of postharvest crop losses, to cite some of the key areas.

In the absence of a dramatic increase in agricultural research, the already diminishing backlog of unused agricultural technology will continue to shrink. Even if there is little prospect of a new technology that would bring a quantum jump in world food production, such as those that came with the discovery of fertilizer or the hybridization of corn, every new technology that would lead to even a small expansion in food output is valuable—and far more so now than in the past, when surpluses reigned.

Similarly, if grain prices rise, the return on investing in measures to reduce losses of grain in storage in Third World villages will also rise. New, synthetic materials that are designed for small-scale storage hold out the hope of reducing such losses.

The shift to scarcity will affect land use policy. During the last half-century, when the world was plagued with farm surpluses and farmers were paid to idle cropland, there seemed little need to worry about the conversion of cropland to nonfarm uses. Cropland was a surplus commodity. But in a world of food scarcity, land use suddenly emerges as a central issue. Already, a group of leading scientists in China has issued a White Paper challenging the decision by the Ministry of Heavy Industry to develop an auto-centered transport system, arguing that the country does not have enough land both to provide roads, highways, and parking lots and to feed its people. They argue instead for a state-of-the-art rail passenger system augmented by bicycles.[119]

Perhaps the best model of successful cropland protection is Japan. The determination to protect its riceland with land-use zoning can be seen in the hundreds of small rice fields within the city boundaries of Tokyo. By tenaciously protecting its riceland, Japan remains self-sufficient in this basic staple.

In addition to protecting cropland from conversion to nonfarm uses, either through zoning or through a stiff tax on conversion, future food security depends on reducing the loss of topsoil from wind and water erosion. In a world facing food scarcity, every ton of topsoil lost from erosion today threatens the food security of the next generation. Here the United States, with its Conservation Reserve Program, has emerged as a leader. Among other things, it promotes the conversion of highly erodible cropland into grass, converting it to grazing land before it becomes wasteland. This program also denies farmers with excessive soil erosion on their land the benefits of any government pro-grams if they do not adopt an approved soil conservation management program to check soil erosion.

Like land, water is also being diverted to nonfarm uses. With water scarcity now constraining efforts to expand food production in many countries, raising the efficiency of water use is emerging as a key to expanding food produc-tion. A shift to water markets, requiring users to pay the full cost of water, would lead to substantial investments in effi-ciency. The common practice of supplying water either free of charge or at a nominal cost to farmers, industries, and urban dwellers leads to water waste.[120]

Securing future food supplies will affect every facet of human existence.

Stretching water supplies enough to satisfy future food needs means boosting the efficiency of water use, emulating the achievements of Israel—the pacesetter in this field. Land productivity has long been part of our vocabulary, an indicator that we measure in yield per hectare. But the term water productivity is rarely heard. Until it too becomes part of our everyday lexicon, water scarcity will cloud our future.

Securing future food supplies will affect every facet of human existence—from land use policy to water use policy to how we use leisure time. If food security is the goal, then the dream of some of having a car in every garage, a swim-ming pool in every backyard, and a golf course in every community may remain simply a dream.

The time may have come for national governments to begin assessing the merit of continuing to use cropland for the production of nonessential crops. For example, the 5 million hectares of cropland used to produce tobacco could produce 15 million tons of grain, enough to cover popula-tion growth for seven months. The grain used in the United States for the production of ethanol as an automobile fuel is not essential and, if phased out, could provide an addition-al 10 million tons of grain for human consumption, enough to cover world population growth for nearly five months.[121]

Until recently, the world had three reserves it could call on in the event of a poor harvest—cropland idled under farm programs, surplus stocks of grain in storage, and the one third of the world grain harvest that is fed to livestock, poultry, and fish. As of 1997, the first two of these reserves have largely disappeared. The only one remaining that can be tapped in a world food emergency is the grain used as feed. This is much more difficult to draw on. Higher prices, of course, will encourage the world's affluent to eat less grain-intensive livestock products, but prices high enough to have this effect also threaten the survival of the world's low-income consumers.

In the event of a world food emergency, one way to restrict the rise in grain prices and restore market stability would be to levy a tax on the consumption of livestock products, offsetting it with a reduction in income taxes. Lowering the demand for grain would also lower its price. Unpopular though it would be, such a tax might be politically acceptable if it were the key to maintaining political stability and sustaining economic progress in low-income countries. Such a step would not solve the food problem, but as a temporary measure it would buy some additional time to stabilize population.

If this analysis is at all close to the mark, future food security depends on creating an environmentally sustainable economy. Simply put, if political leaders do manage to secure food supplies for the next generation, it will be because they have moved the world economy off the current path of environmental deterioration and eventual economic disruption and onto an economic and demographic path that is environmentally sustainable. The purpose of this paper is to convince national political leaders that such an effort is needed.

Notes

1.   World Bank, *Food Security for the World*, statement prepared for the World Food Summit by the World Bank, 12 November 1996. For useful discussions of the connection between environmental degradation and political stability, see Thomas F. Homer-Dixon, Jeffrey H. Boutwell, and George W. Rathjens, "Environmental Change and Violent Conflict," *Scientific American*, February 1993, and Robert D. Kaplan, "The Coming Anarchy," *Atlantic Monthly*, February 1994.

2.   Caroline Southey, "EU Puts New Curbs on Fishing," *Financial Times*, 16 April 1997; grain data from U.S. Department of Agriculture (USDA), *Production, Supply, and Distribution*, electronic database, Washington, DC, updated February 1997.

3.   Kazakstan data from U.N. Food and Agriculture Organization (FAO), *The State of Food and Agriculture 1995*, FAO Agricultural Series No. 28 (Rome: 1995); Brazil's grain data from USDA, Foreign Agricultural Service (FAS), *Grain: World Markets and Trade* (Washington, DC: April 1997).

4.   U.S. Bureau of the Census, *International Data Base*, electronic database, Suitland, MD, 15 May 1996; 800 million figure from World Bank, op. cit. note 1.

5. Susan Cotts Watkins and Jane Menken, "Famines in Historical Perspective," *Population and Development Review*, December 1985.

6.   Oceanic fish catch from FAO, *Yearbook of Fishery Statistics: Catches and Landings* (Rome: 1967–91); 1950–59 grain data from USDA, "World Grain Database," unpublished printout, Washington, DC, 1991; 1960–90 grain data from USDA, op. cit. note 2; current grain data from USDA, FAS, *World Agricultural Production* (Washington, DC: April 1997).

7.   Information on idled cropland from K.F. Isherwood and K.G. Soh, "Short Term Prospects for World Agriculture and Fertilizer Use," presented at 21st Enlarged Council Meeting, International Fertilizer Industry Association, Paris, 15–17 November 1995, and from USDA, FAS, *World Agricultural Production* (Washington, DC: October 1995); data on world carryover stocks of grain from USDA, op. cit. note 2, and USDA, FAS, *Grain: World Markets and Trade* (Washington, DC: July 1997).

8.   "Grain Prices Continue to Climb; Official Urges Calmer Trading," *New York Times*, 26 April 1996; "Prices for Wheat and Corn Drop on Hopes for Improved Harvests," *New York Times*, 30 April 1996; "Futures Prices," *Wall Street Journal*, various editions.

9.   Serge Schmemann, "In Jordan, Bread-Price Protests Signal Deep Anger," *New York Times*, 21 August 1996.

10. Lester R. Brown, *Who Will Feed China? Wake-Up Call for a Small Planet* (New York: W.W. Norton & Company, 1995); USDA, op. cit. note 2; Jack A. Goldstone, "The Coming Chinese Collapse," *Foreign Policy*, Summer 1995.

11. Bureau of the Census, op. cit. note 4; USDA, op. cit. note 3.

12. International Monetary Fund (IMF), *World Economic Outlook, October 1996* (Washington, DC: 1996); Bureau of the Census, op. cit. note 4; USDA, op. cit. note 2; USDA, FAS, *Livestock and Poultry: World Markets and Trade* (Washington, DC: October 1995).

13. Grain-to-beef conversion ratio based on Allen Baker, Feed Situation and Outlook Staff, Economic Research Service (ERS), USDA, Washington, DC, discussion with author, 27 April 1992; grain-to-pork conversion from Leland Southard, Livestock and Poultry Situation and Outlook Staff, ERS, USDA, Washington, DC, discussion with author, 27 April 1992; egg conversion ratios from Alan B. Durning and Holly B. Brough, *Taking Stock: Animal Farming and the Environment*, Worldwatch Paper 103 (Washington, DC: Worldwatch Institute, July 1991); grain-to-poultry ratio derived from Robert V. Bishop et al., *The World Poultry Market—Government Intervention and Multilateral Policy Reform* (Washington, DC: USDA, 1990).

14. Seafood data from FAO, op. cit. note 6; 1950–84 beef and pork data from FAO, *1948–1985 World Crop and Livestock Statistics* (Rome: 1987); 1985–90 beef and pork data from FAO, *FAO Production Yearbooks 1988–1991* (Rome: 1991–1993); recent growth in beef and pork from USDA, FAS, *Livestock and Poultry: World Markets and Trade* (Washington, DC: October 1996).

15. Poultry, pork, mutton, and beef data from FAO, *FAO Production Yearbooks* (Rome: various years), and from USDA, op. cit. note 14; egg and cheese data from FAO, "FAOSTAT DATA," <http://apps.fao.org/lim500/nph-wrap.pl?Production. Livestock.Primary&Domain=SUA>; aquaculture data from FAO, *Aquaculture Production Statistics, 1985–1994*, FAO Fisheries Circular No. 815, Rev. 8 (Rome: 1996), and from Maurizio Perotti, fishery statistician, Fishery Information, Data, and Statistics Unit (FIDI), Fisheries Department, FAO, Rome, letter to Worldwatch, 8 November 1996.

16. USDA, op. cit. note 14; FAO, "FAOSTAT DATA," op. cit. note 15.

17. United Nations, *The Future Growth of World Population*, Population Studies No. 28 (New York: 1958); IMF, op. cit. note 12.

18. IMF, op. cit. note 12; Bureau of the Census, op. cit. note 4; feed data from USDA, op. cit. note 2, and from USDA, FAS, *Grain: World Markets and Trade* (Washington, DC: May 1997).

19. IMF, op. cit. note 12; broiler and milk data from USDA, op. cit. note 14; egg data from FAO, "FAOSTAT DATA", op. cit. note 15; population data from Bureau of the Census, op. cit. note 4; feed grain data from USDA, op. cit. note 2, and from USDA, op. cit. note 3.

20. USDA, op. cit. note 14.

21. USDA, op. cit. note 2; USDA, op. cit. note 3.

22. FAO, op. cit. note 6; Perotti, op. cit. note 15; Bureau of the Census, op. cit. note 4.

23. FAO, op. cit. note 6; USDA, op. cit. note 14.

24. FAO, op. cit. note 6; Bishop et al., op. cit. note 13.

25. USDA, unpublished printout, op. cit. note 6; USDA, op. cit. note 2.

26. USDA, unpublished printout, op cit. note 6; USDA, op. cit. note 2; recent data from USDA, op. cit. note 3; Bureau of the Census, op. cit. note 4.

27. USDA, op. cit. note 2; USDA, July 1997, op. cit. note 7.

28. Isherwood and Soh, op. cit. note 7; USDA, October 1995, op. cit. note 7; USDA, op. cit. note 3.

29. USDA, op. cit. note 2; USDA, FAS, *World Agricultural Production* (Washington, DC: various issues); USDA, FAS, *Grain: World Markets and Trade*, Washington, DC, August 1995; grain price information from IMF, *International Financial Statistics* (Washington, DC: various years).

30. USDA, July 1997, op. cit. note 7; USDA, op. cit. note 2.

31. IMF, *International Statistics Yearbook* (Washington, DC: 1996).

32. "Agriculture and Development," *National Conditions Report No. 5*, National Conditions Analysis and Research Group, Chinese Academy of Sciences, received from Wang Yi, Associate Professor, Chinese Academy of Sciences, Washington, DC, 1 July 1997.

33. Bureau of the Census, op. cit. note 4.

34. USDA, unpublished printout, op. cit. note 6, USDA, op. cit. note 2.

35. USDA, unpublished printout, op. cit. note 6; USDA, op. cit. note 2.

36. USDA, ERS, *Agricultural Resources: Cropland, Water and Conservation Situation and Outlook Report* (Washington, DC: September 1991).

37. FAO, op. cit. note 3.

38. "Chinese Roads Paved with Gold," *Financial Times*, 23 November 1994.

39. N. Vasuki Rao, "World's Top Automakers On the Road to India," *Journal of Commerce*, 26 February 1996.

40. FAO, *FAO Production Yearbooks*, op. cit. note 15; USDA, op. cit. note 2; USDA, FAS, *Oilseeds: World Markets and Trade* (Washington, DC: April 1997).

41. USDA, op. cit. note 2; Wang Rong, "Food Before Golf on Southern Land," *China Daily*, 25 January 1995.

42. USDA, op. cit. note 2.

43. Ibid.; Bureau of the Census, op. cit. note 4.

44. Isherwood and Soh, op. cit. note 7; USDA, October 1995, op. cit. note 7; USDA, FAS, *World Agricultural Production* (Washington, DC: December 1995); USDA, FAS, *World Agricultural Production* (Washington, DC: September 1996); USDA, ERS, *Agricultural Resources Inputs: Situation and Outlook Report* (Washington, DC: October 1993).

45. USDA, unpublished printout, op. cit. note 6; USDA, op. cit. note 2; USDA, op. cit. note 3; population from Bureau of the Census, op. cit. note 4.

46. FAO, *FAO Production Yearbook 1993* (Rome: 1994); Bill Quinby, ERS, USDA, Washington, DC, discussion with author, 24 January 1996.

47. Sandra Postel, *Last Oasis: Facing Water Scarcity* (New York: W.W. Norton & Company, 1992); FAO, *FAO Production Yearbooks*, op. cit. note 15; Quinby, op. cit. note 46.

48. Irrigated area in FAO, *FAO Production Yearbooks*, op. cit. note 15, with per capita figures derived from Bureau of the Census, op. cit. note 4.

49. FAO, *FAO Production Yearbook 1995* (Rome: 1996).

50. W. Hunter Colby et al., *Agricultural Statistics of the People's Republic of China, 1949–90* (Washington, DC: USDA, ERS, 1992).

51. Gordon Sloggett and Clifford Dickason, *Ground-Water Mining in the United States* (Washington, DC: USDA, ERS, 1986).

52. USDA, Natural Resources Conservation Service, *Summary Report: 1992 National Resources Inventory* (Washington, DC: July 1994, rev. January 1995); Sandra Postel, "Forging a Sustainable Water Strategy," in Lester R. Brown et al., *State of the World 1996* (New York: W.W. Norton & Company, 1996).

53. R.P.S. Malik and Paul Faeth, "Rice-Wheat Production in Northwest India," in Paul Faeth, ed., *Agricultural Policy and Sustainability: Case Studies* *from India, Chile, the Philippines, and the United States* (Washington, DC: World Resources Institute, 1993).

54. Professor Chen Yiyu, Chinese Academy of Sciences, Beijing, China, discussion with author, 12 March 1996.

55. Ibid.

56. USDA, op. cit. note 52; Postel, op. cit. note 52; Charles J. Hanley, "Saudi Arabia Farming Sucks the Country Dry," *Associated Press*, 29 March 1997; USDA, op. cit. note 2.

57. McVean Trading and Investments, Memphis, Tenn., discussion with author, 29 May 1996.

58. USDA, op. cit. note 52; Postel, op. cit. note 52.

59. FAO, *Yield Response to Water* (Rome: various years).

60. John Barham, "Euphrates Power Plant Generates New Tension," *Financial Times*, 15 February 1996; Yuan Shu, "Nations Find Unity in Taming the Mekong," *The WorldPaper*, November 1994.

61. David Seckler, *The New Era of Water Resources Management: From 'Dry' to 'Wet' Water Savings*, Issues in Agriculture 8 (Washington, DC: Consultative Group on International Agricultural Research, April 1996).

62. FAO, *FAO Production Yearbooks*, op. cit. note 15; Quinby, op. cit. note 46; Bureau of the Census, op. cit. note 4.

63. USDA, op. cit. note 3.

64. World water use from I.A. Shiklomanov, "Global Water Resources," *Nature & Resources*, Vol. 26, No. 3. 1990.

65. USDA, op. cit. note 2; USDA, FAS, op. cit. note 6.

66. Lester R. Brown, *Increasing World Food Output: Problems and Prospects*, Foreign Agriculture Economic Report No. 25 (Washington, DC: USDA, ERS, April 1965); USDA, op. cit. note 2; USDA, FAS, op. cit. note 6; Japanese price supports from Scott Thompson, FAS, USDA, Washington, DC, discussion with author, 8 July 1997.

67. Brown, op. cit. note 66; USDA, op. cit. note 2; USDA, FAS, op. cit. note 6.

68. L.T. Evans, "The Natural History of Crop Yields," *American Scientist*, July–August, 1980; L.T. Evans, *Crop Evolution, Adaptation, and Yield* (Cambridge, UK: Cambridge University Press, 1993).

69. Evans, "The Natural History of Crop Yields," op. cit. note 68; Evans, *Crop Evolution, Adaptation, and Yield*, op. cit. note 68.

70. Donald N. Duvick, Affiliate Professor of Plant Breeding, Iowa State University, letter to author, 14 March 1997.

71. FAO, *Fertilizer Yearbook* (Rome: various years); K.G. Soh and K.F. Isherwood, "Short Term Prospects for World Agriculture and Fertilizer Use," presentation at IFA Enlarged Council Meeting, International Fertilizer Industry Association, Marrakech, Morocco, 19–22 November 1996.

72. FAO, op. cit. note 71; Isherwood and Soh, op. cit. note 7.

73. Lester R. Brown, *Seeds of Change* (New York: Praeger Publishers, 1970).

74. Duvick, op. cit. note 70.

75. USDA, unpublished printout, op. cit. note 6; USDA, op. cit. note 2; USDA, FAS, op. cit. note 6.

76. USDA, FAS, op. cit. note 6; FAO, op. cit. note 3.

77. USDA, unpublished printout, op. cit. note 6; USDA, op. cit. note 2; USDA, FAS, op. cit. note 6.

78. USDA, unpublished printout, op. cit. note 6; USDA, op. cit. note 2; USDA, FAS, op. cit. note 6.

79. USDA, unpublished printout, op. cit. note 6; USDA, op. cit. note 2; USDA, FAS, op. cit. note 6.

80. Mary Cabrera, International Rice Research Institute, Philippines, letter to Worldwatch, 26 February 1997.

81. Donald O. Mitchell and Merlinda D. Ingco, International Economics Department, *The World Food Outlook* (Washington, DC: World Bank, 1993).

82. Brown, op. cit. note 73; USDA, op. cit. note 3.

83. USDA, unpublished printout, op. cit. note 6; USDA, op. cit. note 2; USDA, FAS, op. cit. note 6.

84. Fredrick W. Crook and Hunter Colby, *The Future of China's Grain Market*, USDA, ERS, Agriculture Information Bulletin Number 730, October 1996; USDA, FAS, op. cit. note 6.

85. USDA, unpublished printout, op. cit. note 6; USDA, op. cit. note 2; USDA, FAS, op. cit. note 6.

86. Gurdev S. Khush, "Modern Varieties—Their Real Contribution to Food Supply and Equity," *GeoJournal*, March 1995.

87. USDA, FAS, op. cit. note 6; USDA, op. cit. note 3.

88. USDA, unpublished printout, op. cit. note 6; USDA, op. cit. note 2; USDA, FAS, op. cit. note 6.

89. USDA, op. cit. note 2; USDA, FAS, op. cit. note 6.

90. USDA, FAS, op. cit. note 6; Soh and Isherwood, op. cit. note 71.

91. USDA, unpublished printout, op. cit. note 6; USDA, op. cit. note 2; USDA, FAS, op. cit. note 6.

92. USDA, unpublished printout op. cit. note 6; USDA, op. cit. note 2; USDA, FAS, op. cit. note 6.

93. Thomas R. Sinclair, "Limits to Crop Yield?" in American Society of Agronomy, Crop Science Society of America, and Soil Science Society of America, *Physiology and Determination of Crop Yield* (Madison, WI: 1994).

94. Brown, op. cit. note 66; USDA, op. cit. note 2; USDA, FAS, op. cit. note 6.

95. USDA, op. cit. note 2.

96. Ibid.; USDA, unpublished printout, op. cit. note 6.

97. USDA, op. cit. note 3; USDA, op. cit. note 2; USDA, unpublished printout, op. cit. note 6.

98. James Hansen et al., Goddard Institute for Space Studies Surface Air Temperature Analyses, "Table of Global-Mean Monthly, Annual and Seasonal Land-Ocean Temperature Index, 1950–Present," <http://www.giss.nasa,gov/Data/GISTEMP>, 19 January 1996; USDA, op. cit. note 2.

99. USDA, op. cit. note 2.

100. USDA, December 1995, op. cit. note 44.

101. "Vietnam to Limit Exports of Rice for Four Months," *Journal of Commerce*, 19 May 1995; information on China from Christopher Goldthwaite, FAS, USDA, Washington, DC, letter to Worldwatch, 25 April 1995; "Wheat Soars to 15-Year High As Europe Puts Tax on Exports," *New York Times*, 8 December 1995; "EU to Conserve Barley by Curbing Exports," *Journal of Commerce*, 12 January 1996.

102. Laurie Morse and Gary Mead, "EU Tax News Boosts Wheat," *Financial Times*, 25 April 1997.

103. FAO, *Food Outlook*, August/September 1995; Shalha Shipouri and Margaret Missiaen, "Shortfalls in International Food Aid Expected," *FoodReview*, September–December 1995.

104. USDA, op. cit. note 3.

105. Bureau of the Census, op. cit. note 4; USDA, op. cit. note 3.

106. United Nations, *World Population Prospects: The 1996 Revision* (New York: forthcoming).

107. Brown, op. cit. note 10.

108. Bureau of the Census, op. cit. note 4.

109. Ibid.; USDA, op. cit. note 3.

110. USDA, op. cit. note 3; Bureau of the Census, op. cit. note 4.

111. Merlinda D. Ingco, Donald O. Mitchell, and Alex F. McCalla, *Global Food Supply Prospects*, World Bank Technical Paper No. 353 (Washington, DC: World Bank, 1996); FAO, *World Agriculture: Towards 2010* (New York: John Wiley & Sons, 1995); "Grain Prices Could Double by 2010," *Kyodo News*, 25 December 1995; "Big Rise in Grain Price Predicted," *China Daily*, 26 December 1995.

112. FAO, *Rome Declaration on World Food Security and World Food Summit Plan of Action*, Rome, 13–17 November 1996.

113. USDA, July 1997, op. cit. note 7.

114. USDA, ERS, "Food Costs Review 1995," *Agricultural Economic Report 729* (Washington, DC: April, 1996); David Harvey, Poultry Specialist, ERS, USDA, discussion with Worldwatch, 1 July 1997.

115. World Bank, op. cit. note 1; 70 percent figure from U.N. Development Programme, *Human Development Report 1993* (New York: Oxford University Press, 1993).

116. U.S. Bureau of the Census, *World Population Profile: 1996* (Washington, DC: U.S. Government Printing Office, July 1996).

117. Unmet need for family planning from U.N. General Assembly, "Draft Programme of Action of the International Conference on Population and Development" (draft), New York, April 1994.

118. Worldwatch estimate based on United Nations, *Energy Statistics Yearbook* (New York: 1996); Christopher Flavin, "Wind Power Growth Continues," and Molly O'Meara, "Solar Cell Shipments Keep Rising," both in Lester R. Brown, Michael Renner, and Christopher Flavin, *Vital Signs 1997* (New York: W.W. Norton & Company, 1997).

119. Patrick E. Tyler, "China's Transport Gridlock: Cars vs. Mass Transit," *New York Times*, 4 May 1996.

120. Postel, op. cit. note 47.

121. USDA, op. cit. note 2; Bureau of the Census, op. cit. note 4.

PUBLICATION ORDER FORM

_____ *State of the World:* **$13.95**
The annual book used by journalists, activists, scholars, and policymakers worldwide to get a clear picture of the environmental problems we face.

_____ *Vital Signs:* **$12.00**
The book of trends that are shaping our future in easy to read graph and table format, with a brief commentary on each trend.

_____ **Subscription to WORLD WATCH magazine: $20.00 (international airmail $35.00)**
Stay abreast of global environmental trends and issues with our award-winning, eminently readable bimonthly magazine.

_____ **Worldwatch Library: $30.00 (international subscribers $45)**
Receive *State of the World* and all Worldwatch Papers as they are released during the calendar year.

_____ **Worldwatch Database Disk Subscription: $89.00**
Contains global agricultural, energy, economic, environmental, social, and military indicators from all current Worldwatch publications including this Paper. Includes a mid-year update, and *Vital Signs* and *State of the World* as they are published. Can be used with Lotus 1-2-3, Quattro Pro, Excel, SuperCalc and many other spreadsheets. **Check one:** _____ **IBM-compatible or** _____ **Macintosh**

_____ **Worldwatch Papers—See complete list on following page**
Single copy: $5.00 • 2–5: $4.00 ea. • 6–20: $3.00 ea. • 21 or more: $2.00 ea. (Call Director of Communication, at (202) 452-1999, for discounts on larger orders.)

$4.00 Shipping and Handling *($8.00 outside North America)*

_____ **TOTAL**

Make check payable to Worldwatch Institute
1776 Massachusetts Ave., NW, Washington, DC 20036-1904 USA

Enclosed is my check or purchase order for U.S. $_____

☐ AMEX ☐ VISA ☐ MasterCard _____
$\qquad\qquad\qquad\qquad\qquad$ Card Number $\qquad\qquad\qquad\qquad$ Expiration Date

_____
name $\qquad\qquad\qquad\qquad\qquad\qquad\qquad$ **daytime phone #**

_____
address

_____
city $\qquad\qquad\qquad\qquad\qquad\qquad$ **state** $\qquad$ **zip/country**

phone: (202) 452-1999   fax: (202) 296-7365   e-mail: wwpub@worldwatch.org
website: www.worldwatch.org

☐ **Send me a brochure of all Worldwatch publications.**

Worldwatch Papers

No. of Copies

_____ 94. **Clearing the Air: A Global Agenda** by Hilary F. French
_____ 95. **Apartheid's Environmental Toll** by Alan B. Durning
_____ 96. **Swords Into Plowshares: Converting to a Peace Economy** by Michael Renner
_____ 97. **The Global Politics of Abortion** by Jodi L. Jacobson
_____ 98. **Alternatives to the Automobile: Transport for Livable Cities** by Marcia D. Lowe
_____ 100. **Beyond the Petroleum Age: Designing a Solar Economy** by Christopher Flavin
and Nicholas Lenssen
_____ 101. **Discarding the Throwaway Society** by John E. Young
_____ 102. **Women's Reproductive Health: The Silent Emergency** by Jodi L. Jacobson
_____ 104. **Jobs in a Sustainable Economy** by Michael Renner
_____ 105. **Shaping Cities: The Environmental and Human Dimensions** by Marcia D. Lowe
_____ 106. **Nuclear Waste: The Problem That Won't Go Away** by Nicholas Lenssen
_____ 107. **After the Earth Summit: The Future of Environmental Governance**
by Hilary F. French
_____ 109. **Mining the Earth** by John E. Young
_____ 110. **Gender Bias: Roadblock to Sustainable Development** by Jodi L. Jacobson
_____ 111. **Empowering Development: The New Energy Equation** by Nicholas Lenssen
_____ 112. **Guardians of the Land: Indigenous Peoples and the Health of the Earth**
by Alan Thein Durning
_____ 113. **Costly Tradeoffs: Reconciling Trade and the Environment** by Hilary F. French
_____ 114. **Critical Juncture: The Future of Peacekeeping** by Michael Renner
_____ 115. **Global Network: Computers in a Sustainable Society** by John E. Young
_____ 116. **Abandoned Seas: Reversing the Decline of the Oceans** by Peter Weber
_____ 117. **Saving the Forests: What Will It Take?** by Alan Thein Durning
_____ 118. **Back on Track: The Global Rail Revival** by Marcia D. Lowe
_____ 119. **Powering the Future: Blueprint for a Sustainable Electricity Industry**
by Christopher Flavin and Nicholas Lenssen
_____ 120. **Net Loss: Fish, Jobs, and the Marine Environment** by Peter Weber
_____ 121. **The Next Efficiency Revolution: Creating a Sustainable Materials Economy**
by John E. Young and Aaron Sachs
_____ 122. **Budgeting for Disarmament: The Costs of War and Peace** by Michael Renner
_____ 123. **High Priorities: Conserving Mountain Ecosystems and Cultures**
by Derek Denniston
_____ 124. **A Building Revolution: How Ecology and Health Concerns Are Transforming
Construction** by David Malin Roodman and Nicholas Lenssen
_____ 125. **The Hour of Departure: Forces That Create Refugees and Migrants** by Hal Kane
_____ 126. **Partnership for the Planet: An Environmental Agenda for the United Nations**
by Hilary F. French
_____ 127. **Eco-Justice: Linking Human Rights and the Environment** by Aaron Sachs
_____ 128. **Imperiled Waters, Impoverished Future: The Decline of Freshwater Ecosystems**
by Janet N. Abramovitz
_____ 129. **Infecting Ourselves: How Environmental and Social Disruptions Trigger Disease**
by Anne E. Platt
_____ 130. **Climate of Hope: New Strategies for Stabilizing the World's Atmosphere**
by Christopher Flavin and Odil Tunali
_____ 131. **Shrinking Fields: Cropland Loss in a World of Eight Billion** by Gary Gardner
_____ 132. **Dividing the Waters: Food Security, Ecosystem Health, and the New Politics of
Scarcity** by Sandra Postel
_____ 133. **Paying the Piper: Subsidies, Politics, and the Environment** by David Malin Roodman
_____ 134. **Getting the Signals Right: Tax Reform to Protect the Environment and the Economy**
by David Malin Roodman
_____ 135. **Recycling Organic Waste: From Urban Pollutant to Farm Resource** by Gary Gardner
_____ 136. **The Agricultural Link: How Environmental Deterioration Could Disrupt Economic
Progress** by Lester R. Brown

_____ **Total copies (transfer number to order form on previous page)**